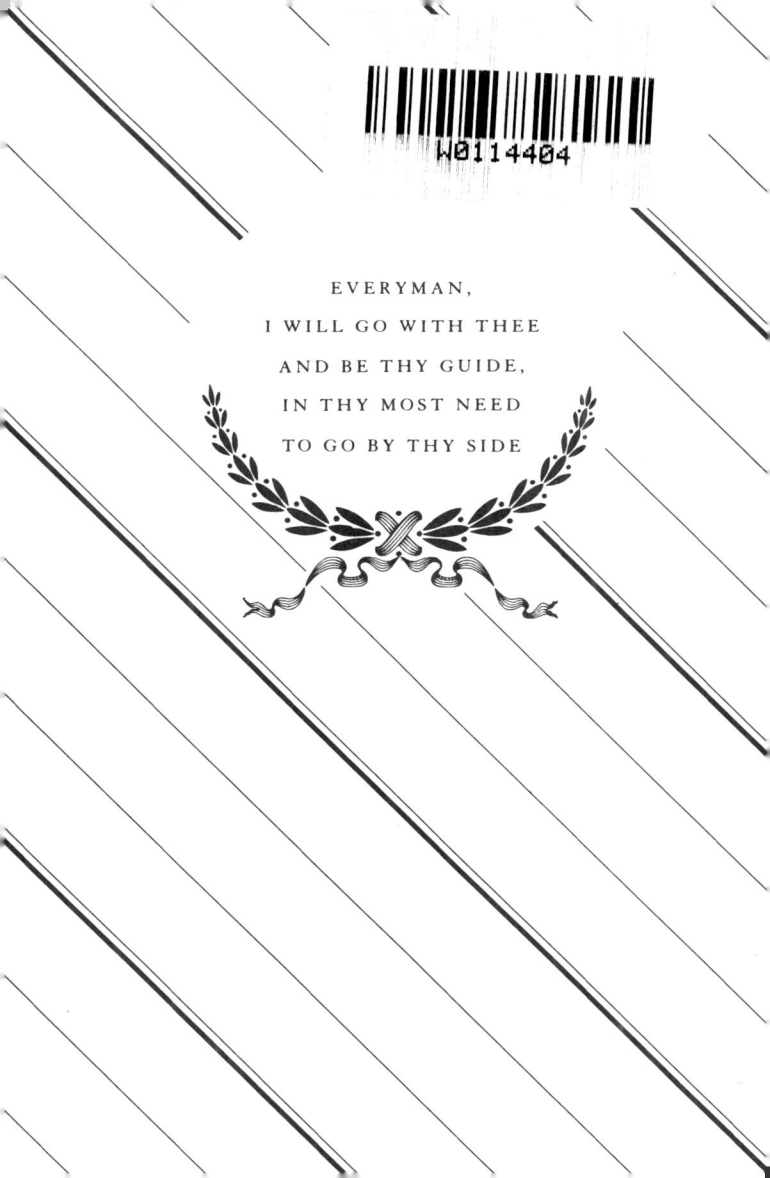

EVERYMAN,
I WILL GO WITH THEE
AND BE THY GUIDE,
IN THY MOST NEED
TO GO BY THY SIDE

EVERYMAN'S LIBRARY
POCKET POETS

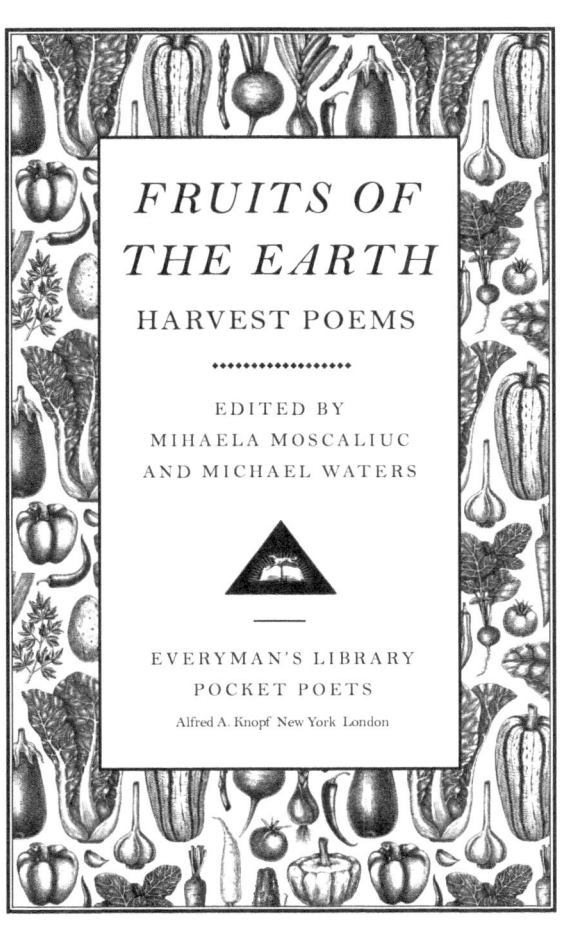

FRUITS OF THE EARTH
HARVEST POEMS

••••••••••••••••••

EDITED BY
MIHAELA MOSCALIUC
AND MICHAEL WATERS

EVERYMAN'S LIBRARY
POCKET POETS

Alfred A. Knopf New York London

THIS IS A BORZOI BOOK
PUBLISHED BY ALFRED A. KNOPF

This selection by Mihaela Moscaliuc and Michael Waters first published
in Everyman's Library, 2025
Copyright © 2025 by Everyman's Library

A list of acknowledgments to copyright owners appears at the back
of this volume.

Published in the United States by Alfred A. Knopf, a division of
Penguin Random House LLC, 1745 Broadway, New York, NY 10019.
Published in the United Kingdom by Everyman's Library, 50 Albemarle
Street, London W1S 4BD and distributed by Penguin Random House
UK, One Embassy Gardens, 8 Viaduct Gardens, London SW11 7BW.

everymanslibrary.com.   penguinrandomhouse.com
www.everymanslibrary.co.uk

ISBN 979-8-217-00718-9 (US)
978-1-84159-835-2 (UK)

A CIP catalogue reference for this book is available from the British Library

Typography by Peter B. Willberg and James Sutton

Typeset in the UK by Input Data Services Ltd, Bridgwater, Somerset

Printed and bound in Germany by GGP Media GmbH, Pössneck

The authorized representative in the EU for product safety and compliance is
Penguin Random House Ireland, Morrison Chambers, 32 Nassau Street, Dublin
D02 YH68, Ireland, https://eu-contact.penguin.ie

CONTENTS

6

VEGETABLES

8

9

10

FOREWORD

In several early (2nd–4th centuries) versions of the lives of Adam and Eve, after joining Eve in tasting the forbidden fruit, the expulsed Adam was granted permission to take four spices from Paradise – crocus, nard, reed, and cinnamon. Centuries later, we still carry memories of gardens lost or imagined, their scents as beckoning as the taste of the fruit (apple, quince, pomegranate, as different mythologies have it) said to have deprived us of a divine existence in exchange for an earthly one. What the latter has offered us is nothing less than miraculous, and perhaps no less enticing than the garden in *Song of Solomon*: "My beloved is gone down into his garden, to the beds of spices, to feed in the gardens."

Through its bounty of fruits, vegetables, grains, and culinary herbs and spices, the earth has given us a home in exile, and might continue to do so for as long as we care for it. When its output suffers, for reasons within or beyond our control, we all suffer. We plow, sow, and harvest it to nourish ourselves and others. In cultivating the earth, in growing gardens and orchards, we also cultivate care and community. The 21st-century emergence of community gardens in urban areas, small oases surrounded by concrete and high-rises, speaks to this.

Produce, grains, and spices inform economies and world politics. In the right hands, they cross continents to improve diets and palates, and to acculturate our tastebuds to difference. In greedy hands, these same earthly delights are used for trade and commerce that perpetuate exploitation; empires prosper by subjugating nations and deepening racial inequality. Think of such staples as salt, sugar, and coffee, and how they have shaped human history, from the earlier forms of slavery to current forms of neo-colonial domination.

Whether used with literal or figurative meaning, fruits, vegetables, grains, and spices give shape to a formidable range of sentiments and ideas, from recalling the thrill of biting for the first time into an exotic fruit or inhaling the aromas of a grandmother's curried lentils to finding, in a grain of sugar, the bitter history of cane fields and their legacy of enslavement or indentured labor.

Sometimes the literary meaning of certain fruits and vegetables varies across cultures. Depending on context, a fig might evoke immortality, fertility, holiness, or exile; it may channel both the erotic and the divine. Or it might bring us into the riveting intimacy of a wounding memory. In the work of those who left or were forced out of ancestral lands to seek better lives in America, Europe, and other shores, certain native fruits, vegetables, and spices signify some of the most enduring connections to homeland and heritage.

This collection, which comprises 154 poems by poets from many cultures, is an ode to the earth and its cornucopia, and a reminder of our obligation to honor its generosity. These poems' sensory delights return us, if momentarily, to the abundance of a Paradise we attempt to re-create on earth.

Mihaela Moscaliuc
Michael Waters

FRUITS

INSIDE THE APPLE

You visit me inside the apple.
Together we can hear the knife
paring around and around us, carefully,
so the peel won't tear.

You speak to me. I trust your voice
because it has lumps of hard pain in it
the way real honey
has lumps of wax from the honeycomb.

I touch your lips with my fingers:
that too is a prophetic gesture.
And your lips are red, the way a burnt field
is black.
It's all true.

You visit me inside the apple
and you'll stay with me inside the apple
until the knife finishes its work.

YEHUDA AMICHAI (1924–2000)
TRANSLATED BY CHANA BLOCH and
STEPHEN MITCHELL

ADAM LAY IBOUNDEN

Adam lay ibounden,
　　Bounden in a bond;
Four thousand winter
　　Thoght he not too long;
And all was for an appil,
　　An appil that he tok,
As clerkes finden
　　Wreten in here book.
Ne hadde the appil take ben,
　　The appil taken ben,
Ne hadde never our lady
　　A ben hevene quene.
Blessed be the time
　　That appil take was.
Therefore we moun singen
　　"Deo gracias."

"A QUINCE PRESERVED"

A quince preserved through the winter, given to a lady

I'm a quince, saved over from last year, still fresh,
   my skin young, not spotted or wrinkled, downy as
     the new-born,
as though I were still among my leaves. Seldom
   does winter yield such gifts, but for you, my queen,
even the snows and frosts bear harvests like this.

ANTIPHILOS (1ST CENTURY CE)
TRANSLATED BY W. S. MERWIN

GREEN CHILE

I prefer red chile over my eggs
and potatoes for breakfast.
Red chile *ristras* decorate my door,
dry on my roof, and hang from eaves.
They lend open-air vegetable stands
historical grandeur, and gently swing
with an air of festive welcome.
I can hear them talking in the wind,
haggard, yellowing, crisp, rasping
tongues of old men, licking the breeze.

But our grandmother loves green chile.
When I visit her,
she holds the green chile pepper
in her wrinkled hands.
Ah, voluptuous, masculine,
an air of authority and youth simmers
from its swan-neck stem, tapering to a flowery
collar, fermenting resinous spice.
A well-dressed gentleman at the door
my grandmother takes sensuously in her hand,
rubbing its firm glossed sides,
caressing the oily rubbery serpent,
with mouth-watering fulfillment,
fondling its curves with gentle fingers.

Its bearing magnificent and taut
as flanks of a tiger in mid-leap,
she thrusts her blade into
and cuts it open, with lust
on her hot mouth, sweating over the stove,
bandanna round her forehead,
mysterious passion on her face
as she serves me green chile con carne
between soft warm leaves of corn tortillas,
with beans and rice – her sacrifice
to her little prince.
I slurp from my plate
with last bit of tortilla, my mouth burns
and I hiss and drink a tall glass of cold water.

All over New Mexico, sunburned men and women
drive rickety trucks stuffed with gunny-sacks
of green chile, from Belen, Veguita, Willard, Estancia,
San Antonio y Socorro, from fields
to roadside stands, you see them roasting green chile
in screen-sided homemade barrels, and for a dollar
        a bag,
we relive this old, beautiful ritual again and again.

"I ASKED A THIEF TO STEAL ME A PEACH"

I asked a thief to steal me a peach:
He turned up his eyes.
I ask'd a lithe lady to lie her down:
Holy & meek she cries.

As soon as I went
An angel came:
He wink'd at the thief
And smil'd at the dame,

And without one word said
Had a peach from the tree,
And still as a maid
Enjoy'd the lady.

THE POMEGRANATE

The only legend I have ever loved is
the story of a daughter lost in hell.
And found and rescued there.
Love and blackmail are the gist of it.
Ceres and Persephone the names.
And the best thing about the legend is
I can enter it anywhere. And have.
As a child in exile in
a city of fogs and strange consonants,
I read it first and at first I was
an exiled child in the crackling dusk of
the underworld, the stars blighted. Later
I walked out in a summer twilight
searching for my daughter at bed-time.
When she came running I was ready
to make any bargain to keep her.
I carried her back past whitebeams
and wasps and honey-scented buddleias.
But I was Ceres then and I knew
winter was in store for every leaf
on every tree on that road.
Was inescapable for each one we passed.
And for me.
          It is winter
and the stars are hidden.

I climb the stairs and stand where I can see
my child asleep beside her teen magazines,
her can of Coke, her plate of uncut fruit.
The pomegranate! How did I forget it?
She could have come home and been safe
and ended the story and all
our heart-broken searching but she reached
out a hand and plucked a pomegranate.
She put out her hand and pulled down
the French sound for apple and
the noise of stone and the proof
that even in the place of death,
at the heart of legend, in the midst
of rocks full of unshed tears
ready to be diamonds by the time
the story was told, a child can be
hungry. I could warn her. There is still a chance.
The rain is cold. The road is flint-coloured.
The suburb has cars and cable television.
The veiled stars are above ground.
It is another world. But what else
can a mother give her daughter but such
beautiful rifts in time?
If I defer the grief I will diminish the gift.
The legend will be hers as well as mine.

She will enter it. As I have.
She will wake up. She will hold
the papery flushed skin in her hand.
And to her lips. I will say nothing.

THE APPLES

And what must we think
Of these yellow apples?
Yesterday, they
Astonished, waiting like
This, naked
After the leaves had
Fallen,

Today they charm
As their shoulders
Are modestly accented
With an edging of snow.

YVES BONNEFOY (1923–2016)
TRANSLATED BY SARAH LAWSON

"THERE IS A GARDEN IN HER FACE"

There is a Garden in her face,
Where Roses and white Lillies grow;
A heav'nly paradice is that place,
Wherein all pleasant fruits doe flow.
There Cherries grow, which none may buy
Till Cherry ripe themselves doe cry.

Those Cherries fayrely doe enclose
Of Orient Pearle a double row,
Which when her lovely laughter showes,
They looke like Rose-buds fill'd with snow.
Yet them nor Peere nor Prince can buy,
Till Cherry ripe themselves doe cry.

Her Eyes like Angels watch them still;
Her Browes like bended bowes doe stand,
Threatning with piercing frownes to kill
All that attempt with eye or hand
Those sacred Cherries to come nigh,
Till Cherry ripe themselves doe cry.

THOMAS CAMPION (1567–1620)   29

WINTER FIGS

Winter figs
arrive on branches convulsed by cold.
Tight-shut hard stubborn
unlike their easy-going
summer companions
they're red inside like
an icy sunset with no yellow
wild suspicious
at every rustle of a bough
between sour lips they lock
a streak of sugar.
Arriving unexpected
they leave
the way they came
fragments roaming
in the void in the dark
struck for an instant by the light.

30 BARTOLO CATTAFI (1922–79)
TRANSLATED BY RUTH FELDMAN and
BRIAN SWANN

From THE CANTERBURY TALES
(THE REEVE'S PROLOGUE)

But I am old; a jest suits not my age.
Green days are done; and straw's my forage.
This white head proclaims my aged years;
My heart is as wasted as my hairs,
Unless I too am like the medlars –
The longer the fruit lasts the worse
It is, till rotten, in the dung and straw.
And we old men, I fear, are similar:
Till we be rotten we cannot be ripe.
We jig about as long as men will pipe;
For our will hangs always by this nail,
To have a hoary head and green tail,
As a leek has; and though our strength is gone,
Our will seeks folly ever and anon.

GEOFFREY CHAUCER (*c.* 1343 – 1400)   31
VERSION BY A. S. KLINE

THE ORANGE

At lunchtime I bought a huge orange –
The size of it made us all laugh.
I peeled it and shared it with Robert and Dave –
They got quarters and I had a half.

And that orange, it made me so happy,
As ordinary things often do
Just lately. The shopping. A walk in the park.
This is peace and contentment. It's new.

The rest of the day was quite easy.
I did all the jobs on my list
And enjoyed them and had some time over.
I love you. I'm glad I exist.

GARDEN ABSTRACT

The apple on its bough is her desire, –
Shining suspension, mimic of the sun.
The bough has caught her breath up, and her voice,
Dumbly articulate in the slant and rise
Of branch on branch above her, blurs her eyes.
She is prisoner of the tree and its green fingers.

And so she comes to dream herself the tree,
The wind possessing her, weaving her young veins,
Holding her to the sky and its quick blue,
Drowning the fever of her hands in sunlight.
She has no memory, nor fear, nor hope
Beyond the grass and shadows at her feet.

PEAR TREE

Silver dust
lifted from the earth,
higher than my arms reach,
you have mounted.
O silver,
higher than my arms reach
you front us with great mass;

no flower ever opened
so staunch a white leaf,
no flower ever parted silver
from such rare silver;

O white pear,
your flower-tufts,
thick on the branch,
bring summer and ripe fruits
in their purple hearts.

MOONLIT APPLES

At the top of the house the apples are laid in rows,
And the skylight lets the moonlight in, and those
Apples are deep-sea apples of green. There goes
A cloud on the moon in the autumn night.
A mouse in the wainscot scratches, and scratches,
    and then
There is no sound at the top of the house of men
Or mice; and the cloud is blown, and the moon again
Dapples the apples with deep-sea light.
They are lying in rows there, under the gloomy
    beams;
On the sagging floor; they gather the silver streams
Out of the moon, those moonlit apples of dreams,
And quiet is the steep stair under.
In the corridors under there is nothing but sleep.
And stiller than ever on orchard boughs they keep
Tryst with the moon, and deep is the silence, deep
On moon-washed apples of wonder.

JOHN DRINKWATER (1882 – 1937)

AFTER APPLE-PICKING

My long two-pointed ladder's sticking through a tree
Toward heaven still,
And there's a barrel that I didn't fill
Beside it, and there may be two or three
Apples I didn't pick upon some bough.
But I am done with apple-picking now.
Essence of winter sleep is on the night,
The scent of apples: I am drowsing off.
I cannot rub the strangeness from my sight
I got from looking through a pane of glass
I skimmed this morning from the drinking trough
And held against the world of hoary grass.
It melted, and I let it fall and break.
But I was well
Upon my way to sleep before it fell,
And I could tell
What form my dreaming was about to take.
Magnified apples appear and disappear,
Stem end and blossom end,
And every fleck of russet showing clear.
My instep arch not only keeps the ache,
It keeps the pressure of a ladder-round.
I feel the ladder sway as the boughs bend.
And I keep hearing from the cellar bin
The rumbling sound

Of load on load of apples coming in.
For I have had too much
Of apple-picking: I am overtired
Of the great harvest I myself desired.
There were ten thousand thousand fruit to touch,
Cherish in hand, lift down, and not let fall.
For all
That struck the earth,
No matter if not bruised or spiked with stubble,
Went surely to the cider-apple heap
As of no worth.
One can see what will trouble
This sleep of mine, whatever sleep it is.
Were he not gone,
The woodchuck could say whether it's like his
Long sleep, as I describe its coming on,
Or just some human sleep.

AN APPLE FOR ISAAC

My lord, take this delicacy in your hand.
Smell its fragrance. Forget your longing.
On both sides it blushes, like a young girl
At the first touch of my hand on her breast.
It is an orphan, with no brother, no sister,
Far away from its leafy home.
When it was plucked, its companions were jealous,
They envied its journey, and cried:
"Bear greetings to your master, Isaac.
How lucky you are to be kissed by his lips!"

AUTUMN

And yet, and yet, when the cold
makes brittle what remains – the spent okra
stalk, the few pepper plants that hung on
through the first two frosts, those little gold
tomatoes – when it withers even the rogue
amaranth, its tousled
mane bent and defeated,
when the silver maple out front has ceased
    whispering,
and when the bullfrogs nestle into their muddy lairs,
and the peepers go where they go,
and the crows circle,
just down the street, its leaves
too mostly blown off, spindly
and creaking in the wind,
while the whole world shimmers with death,
hauling all its sugar into perfect globes
the size of a child's handful,
giddy, it seems,
at the sound of ants
slurping beneath, at me
joining them, brushing away wood chip and beetle
before burying my tongue
in the burst pulp
dropped on the earth below,

the persimmon
gives its modest fruit
for yet a while.

THE RASPBERRY ROOM

It was solid hedge, loops of bramble and thorny
as it had to be with its berries thick as bumblebees.
It drew blood just to get there, but I was queen
of that place, at ten, though the berries shook like fists
in the wind, daring anyone to come in. I was trying
so hard to love this world – real rooms too big and full
of worry to comfortably inhabit – but believing
    I was born
to live in that cloistered green bower: the raspberry
    patch
in the back acre of my grandparents' orchard.
    I was cross-
stitched and beaded by its fat, dollmaker's needles.
    The effort
of sliding under the heavy, spiked tangles that tore
my clothes and smeared me with juice was rewarded
with space, wholly mine, a kind of room out of
the crush of the bushes with a canopy of raspberry
dagger-leaves and a syrup of sun and birdsong.
Hours would pass in the loud buzz of it, blood
made it mine – the adventure of that red sting singing
down my calves, the place the scratches brought me to:
just space enough for a girl to lie down.

KARIN GOTTSHALL (1970–)

BLACKBERRY-PICKING
for Philip Hobsbaum

Late August, given heavy rain and sun
For a full week, the blackberries would ripen.
At first, just one, a glossy purple clot
Among others, red, green, hard as a knot.
You ate that first one and its flesh was sweet
Like thickened wine: summer's blood was in it
Leaving stains upon the tongue and lust for
Picking. Then red ones inked up and that hunger
Sent us out with milk cans, pea tins, jam pots
Where briars scratched and wet grass bleached our
          boots.
Round hayfields, cornfields and potato drills
We trekked and picked until the cans were full,
Until the tinkling bottom had been covered
With green ones, and on top big dark blobs burned
Like a plate of eyes. Our hands were peppered
With thorn pricks, our palms sticky as Bluebeard's.

We hoarded the fresh berries in the byre
But when the bath was filled we found a fur,
A rat-grey fungus, glutting on our cache.
The juice was stinking too. Once off the bush
The fruit fermented, the sweet flesh would turn sour.

I always felt like crying. It wasn't fair
That all the lovely canfuls smelt of rot.
Each year I hoped they'd keep, knew they would not.

"YOUR HEART? – IT IS A FROZEN ORANGE"

Your heart? – it is a frozen orange,
inside it has juniper oil but no light
and a porous look like gold: an outside
promising risks to the man who looks.

My heart is a fiery pomegranate,
its scarlets clustered, and its wax opened,
which could offer you its tender beads
with the stubbornness of a man in love.

Yes, what an experience of sorrow it is
to go to your heart and find a frost
made of primitive and terrifying snow!

A thirsty handkerchief flies through the air
along the shores of my weeping,
hoping that he can drink in my tears.

44 MIGUEL HERNÁNDEZ (1910–42)
    TRANSLATED BY ROBERT BLY

CHERRY-RIPE

Cherry-ripe, ripe, ripe, I cry,
Full and fair ones; come and buy.
If so be you ask me where
They do grow, I answer: There
Where my Julia's lips do smile;
There's the land, or cherry-isle,
Whose plantations fully show
All the year where cherries grow.

ROBERT HERRICK (1591 – 1674)   45

GREEN-STRIPED MELONS

They lie
under stars in a field.
They lie under rain in a field.
Under sun.

Some people
are like this as well —
like a painting
hidden beneath another painting.

An unexpected weight
the sign of their ripeness.

From THE ODYSSEY

Thence, o'er the Deep proceeding sad, we reach'd
The land at length, where, giant-sized and free
From all constraint of law, the Cyclops dwell.
They, trusting to the Gods, plant not, or plough,
But earth unsow'd, untill'd, brings forth for them
All fruits, wheat, barley, and the vinous grape
Large cluster'd, nourish'd by the show'rs of Jove.

HOMER (*c.* 8TH CENTURY BCE)   47
TRANSLATED BY WILLIAM COWPER

From BARNFLOOR AND WINEPRESS

And he said, If the Lord do not help thee, whence shall I help
thee? out of the barnfloor, or out of the winepress?

2 Kings VI:27

Thou whose dry plot for moisture gapes,
We shout with them that tread the grapes:
For us the Vine was fenced with thorn,
Five ways the precious branches torn;
Terrible fruit was on the tree
In the acre of Gethsemane;
For us by Calvary's distress
The wine was racked from the press;
Now in our altar-vessels stored
Is the sweet Vintage of our Lord.

In Joseph's garden they threw by
The riv'n Vine, leafless, lifeless, dry:
On Easter morn the Tree was forth,
In forty days reach'd heaven from earth;
Soon the whole world is overspread;
Ye weary, come into the shade.

APPLE DUMPS

After the fiesta, the beauty-contests, the drunken wrestling
Of the blossom
Come some small ugly swellings, the dwarfish truths
Of the prizes.

After blushing and confetti, the breeze-blown
    bridesmaids, the shadowed snapshots
Of the trees in bloom
Come the gruelling knuckles, and the cracked
    housemaid's hands,
The workworn morning plainness of apples.

Unearthly was the hope, the wet star melting the
    gland,
Staggering the offer –
But pawky the real returns, not easy to see,
Dull and leaf-green, hidden, still-bitter, and hard.

The orchard flared wings, a new heaven, a dawn-
    lipped apocalypse
Kissing the sleeper –
The apples emerge, in the sun's black shade, among
    stricken trees,
A straggle of survivors, nearly all ailing.

TED HUGHES (1930–98)   49

APPLES AND MANGOES

The exotic fruit
was placed upon the table
and invited comment:
"I prefer to eat apples at home,"
said the professor from SOAS,
"but when out I like a slice or two
of mango;
that is what it is no doubt?"
"Easy to get hold of these days,"
said the liberal host
who wrote guilt-ridden plays about blacks.
"A transplant, I can see
by its shape and colour,
from India on African soil,"
remarked the social worker from Battersea.
"A good thing surely
in the cause of internationalism,"
muttered the pale bespectacled revolutionary.
"I like its pink blush, subtle
not too obvious in natural light
tastes nice if eaten late at night,"
said the artist, adding,
"Almost nipple like its eye
where all the juice can be sucked through."
"No! No! It's not one you can suck!"

screamed the professor, hands shaking
with age and anticipation as he picked
the knife. "Surely this is one for slicing."
"Some of these mangoes," said the poet,
"look ok but taste like apples
and are the same colour inside."
"Hmm," said the professor as everyone smiled,
"a cross between an apple and a mango!
Science has indeed made great strides."
"Hmm," added everyone as they had a slice.

From TO PENSHURST

Then hath thy orchard fruit, thy garden flowers,
Fresh as the air, and new as are the hours.
The early cherry, with the later plum,
Fig, grape, and quince, each in his time doth come;
The blushing apricot and woolly peach
Hang on thy walls, that every child may reach.
And though thy walls be of the country stone,
They're reared with no man's ruin, no man's groan;
There's none that dwell about them wish them down;
But all come in, the farmer and the clown,
And no one empty-handed, to salute
Thy lord and lady, though they have no suit.
Some bring a capon, some a rural cake,
Some nuts, some apples; some that think they make
The better cheeses bring them, or else send
By their ripe daughters, whom they would commend
This way to husbands, and whose baskets bear
An emblem of themselves in plum or pear.

FRUIT ON THE WINDOWSILL

And then day, rising from the lake's blue depths
Comes to the windows and silence
Takes this form: fruit
Lined up here by chance, while a sweet

Peach's cleft trembles at a reverse angle,
Recalling hours passed drinking air
Warmed in September's unpoisoned crystal.
Hills, and the stream makes its captive sound

Beneath gilt logs, the hour moves forward
On a thread of sun; wild catches
Make the grass dance too, a human being

Reflects that he merely inhabits
Half of himself, but the measure, which is unique,
Keeps him from making a terrace of his regret.

HÉDI KADDOUR (1945–)

TRANSLATED BY MARILYN HACKER

From THE EVE OF ST. AGNES

And still she slept an azure-lidded sleep,
In blanchèd linen, smooth, and lavendered,
While he from forth the closet brought a heap
Of candied apple, quince, and plum, and gourd,
With jellies soother than the creamy curd,
And lucent syrups, tinct with cinnamon;
Manna and dates, in argosy transferred
From Fez; and spicèd dainties, every one,
From silken Samarkand to cedared Lebanon.

BLACKBERRY EATING

I love to go out in late September
among the fat, overripe, icy, black blackberries
to eat blackberries for breakfast,
the stalks very prickly, a penalty
they earn for knowing the black art
of blackberry making; and as I stand among them
lifting the stalks to my mouth, the ripest berries
fall almost unbidden to my tongue,
as words sometimes do, certain peculiar words
like *strengths* or *squinched* or *broughamed*,
many-lettered, one-syllabled lumps,
which I squeeze, squinch open, and splurge well
in the silent, startled, icy, black language
of blackberry eating in late September.

PLUMBURST
for Wendy

The neat greens of Monument Hill
roll into sea, over the rise the soft rain
of plumfall deceives us in its groundburst.

If lightning strikes from the ground up,
and Heaven is but an irritation that prompts
its angry spark, then plums are born
dishevelled on the ground and rise
towards perfection . . .

Out of the range of rising plums
we mark the territory of the garden,
testing caprock with Judas trees,
pacing out melon runs. Behind us a block
of flats hums into dusk and the sun
bursts a plum mid-flight.

BLACKBERRIES

They left my hands like a printer's
Or thief's before a police blotter
& pulled me into early morning's
Terrestrial sweetness, so thick
The damp ground was consecrated
Where they fell among a garland of thorns.

Although I could smell old lime-covered
History, at ten I'd still hold out my hands
& berries fell into them. Eating from one
& filling a half gallon with the other,
I ate the mythology & dreamt
Of pies & cobbler, almost

Needful as forgiveness. My bird dog Spot
Eyed blue jays & thrashers. The mud frogs
In rich blackness, hid from daylight.
An hour later, beside City Limits Road
I balanced a gleaming can in each hand,
Limboed between worlds, repeating *one dollar*.

The big blue car made me sweat.
Wintertime crawled out of the windows.
When I leaned closer I saw the boy
& girl my age, in the wide back seat
Smirking, & it was then I remembered my fingers
Burning with thorns among berries too ripe to touch.

BREADFRUIT

Boys dream of native girls who bring breadfruit,
    Whatever they are,
As brides to teach them how to execute
Sixteen sexual positions on the sand;
This makes them join (the boys) the tennis club,
Jive at the Mecca, use deodorants, and
On Saturdays squire ex-schoolgirls to the pub
    By private car.

Such uncorrected visions end in church
    Or registrar:
A mortgaged semi- with a silver birch;
Nippers; the widowed mum; having to scheme
With money; illness; age. So absolute
Maturity falls, when old men sit and dream
Of naked native girls who bring breadfruit
    Whatever they are.

PHILIP LARKIN (1922–85)   59

CHERRY ROBBERS

Under the long, dark boughs, like jewels red
    In the hair of an Eastern girl
Shine strings of crimson cherries, as if had bled
    Blood-drops beneath each curl.

Under the glistening cherries, with folded wings
    Three dead birds lie:
Pale-breasted throstles and a blackbird, robberlings
    Stained with red dye.

Under the haystack a girl stands laughing at me,
    With cherries hung round her ears –
Offering me her scarlet fruit: I will see
    If she has any tears.

AVOCADO
for Robert Bly

It is a green globe like a vegetable light bulb
with a stem to meet either soil or small living tree;
it is mottled like an old man's face or is wizened
like the enormous head of a fetus. Now the stem
has come away from a navel.
It has the stolid heft of a stone. The smell seeps up
and leads the mind far away to the earth's ancient cave.
Its taste is also pungent dirt with a kind of bark
that is quite difficult to chew:
here is the small tomb of woman.
Mother smells its fresh soil even with her dead sense.
        She feels
its husk. Her body inside is the soft flesh of fruit,
and her heart this oval green core.
Her grief, her anger is that she
no longer has life, but the stuff of her breathes a res-
idue that has remained in earth
and in the minds of the children.
Oh, now I know her skin sighs green
as this fluted fruit: her spirit
is the taste of it, transmuted.

BLACKBERRY BUSH

Blackberry, with the grey stem, give me
a handful of berries to eat.

Blood & thorns.   Closer!
If you love me, I'll love you.

Leave on my tongue your
fruit of green & shadow,   blackberry .

              Just think
of the long hug I'll give you with-
in the partial shadow of my thorns .

Blackberry, where're you going?
To look for the loves you don't give
                              me.

FEDERICO GARCÍA LORCA (1898–1936)
TRANSLATED BY PAUL BLACKBURN

TO PRESERVE FIGS
for Iseult

Go up the whitewashed ladder, by the wall,
       And you'll find seven pounds
    Of them, half-ripened, on the tree.
         The rest were low
I picked before. They wallowed free
        Near to the ground's
Welter of nettles, apples, weeds. I know,
  You'll have to take care. You might fall.

But there are plenty, seven pounds I'd say,
       Still floundering heavy, green
    And solid in the August air,
         And you can reach
Them if you climb. So go up there
        And get them, keen
As fig-juice in your envy. Gather each
  Into your fingers, let none stay,

On the branch. It makes a metaphor for lust,
       This grasping for the rounds
    Of unripe figs that ooze their juice,
        Their sperm. It burns,
That juice, and has no helpful use.
        You'll live with mounds

Of severed energy, with jaded urns
   Whose milked white necks you'll have to trust

Through all your life. It's best you learn that soon.
          The acid in the fruit
      Pickles the world with its pain
            And nothing breaks
     The dour addiction of the brain
         To what may suit,
Or spoil. So watch your mother while she makes
   These tractable. Take up a spoon

And help. Three times they boil, and have to steep,
        Then boil again. Three times
    It always has to be. So let
     Them dry in trays
    In your burning oven. Go and get
      A sugary slime's
Blandishing oil. In winter, black to your gaze,
   Like whales from arctic ice, they'll leap.

"THE SHY SPEECHLESS SOUND"

The shy speechless sound
of a fruit falling from its tree,
and around it the silent music
of the forest, unbroken . . .

OSIP MANDELSTAM (1891 – 1938)
TRANSLATED BY CLARENCE BROWN and
W. S. MERWIN

From THE GARDEN

What wond'rous life in this I lead!
Ripe apples drop about my head;
The luscious clusters of the vine
Upon my mouth do crush their wine;
The nectarine and curious peach
Into my hands themselves do reach;
Stumbling on melons as I pass,
Ensnar'd with flow'rs, I fall on grass.

TWO GRAPEFRUITS

My husband made me juice –
each morning rose and in the kitchen,
in the early light idling through blue glass,
crushed the fruit, palmed it across
the juicer, filtered the pits and pulp and
carried it back to me, rubbing my shoulder
as I drank. My lover
rises early – hours before me –
slices the fruit and with a curved, serrated
knife, dissects each section, carefully separating
the membranes, as they say God first sliced
the person in two – man and woman – so that
each would ache for its other.
I want them both. I want the juice and the meat,
that pure exquisite liquid and the tender
flesh, the reddish pulp. All of it.
If you get the pure juice, you lose
the juicy flesh and if you eat the flesh you miss
the way the juice goes down. So easily.

PLANTING

"Time is longer than rope."
— *Jamaican proverb*

Nights, fog comes in low,
peeling off the ocean's face
like a serpent shedding skin.

In the garden, nothing will grow.
My mother and I
plant cassava, cocoa, and yam.

Under the sun we toil.
At dusk we listen and wait.
But the soil is watered with salt.

And when sea frost
comes in with the tide,
again, our work is undone.

Granny says the land's memory
is long. And a land that knew terror
will yield no fruit.

THE SEED-PICTURE

This is my portrait of Joanna – since the split
The children come to me like a dumb-waiter,
And I wonder where to put them, beautiful seeds
With no immediate application . . . the clairvoyance
Of seed-work has opened up
New spectrums of activity, beyond a second home.
The seeds dictate their own vocabulary,
Their dusty colours capture
More than we can plan,
The mould on walls, or jumbled garages,
Dead flower heads where insects shack . . .
I only guide them not by guesswork
In their necessary numbers,
And attach them by the spine to a perfect bedding,
Woody orange pips, and tear-drop apple,
The banana of the caraway, wrinkled pepper-corns,
The pocked peach, or waterlily honesty,
The seamed cherry stone so hard to break.

Was it such self-indulgence to enclose her
In the border of a grandmother's sampler,
Bonding all the seeds in one continuous skin,
The sky resolved to a cloud the length of a man?
To use tan linseed for the trees, spiky
Sunflower for leaves, bright lentils

For the window, patna stars
For the floral blouse? Her hair
Is made of hook-shaped marigold, gold
Of pleasure for her lips, like raspberry grain.
The eyelids oatmeal, the irises
Of Dutch blue maw, black rape
For the pupils, millet
For the vicious beige circles underneath.
The single pearl barley
That sleeps around her dullness
Till it catches light, makes women
Feel their age, and sigh for liberation.

NEVER MAY THE FRUIT BE PICKED

Never, never may the fruit be plucked from the bough
And gathered into barrels.
He that would eat of love must eat it where it hangs.
Though the branches bend like reeds,
Though the ripe fruit splash in the grass or wrinkle
      on the tree,
He that would eat of love may bear away with him
Only what his belly can hold,
Nothing in the apron,
Nothing in the pockets.
Never, never may the fruit be gathered from the
      bough
And harvested in barrels.
The winter of love is a cellar of empty bins,
In an orchard soft with rot.

From PARADISE LOST

Here grows the Cure of all, this Fruit Divine,
Fair to the Eye, inviting to the Taste,
Of vertue to make wise: what hinders then
To reach, and feed at once both Bodie and Mind?

So saying, her rash hand in evil hour
Forth reaching to the Fruit, she pluck'd, she eat:
Earth felt the wound, and Nature from her seat
Sighing through all her Works gave signs of woe,
That all was lost. Back to the Thicket slunk
The guiltie Serpent, and well might, for *Eve*
Intent now wholly on her taste, naught else
Regarded, such delight till then, as seemd,
In Fruit she never tasted, whether true
Or fansied so, through expectation high
Of knowledg, nor was God-head from her thought.
Greedily she ingorg'd without restraint,
And knew not eating Death.

of betraying their final secret,
sometimes we feel we're about
to uncover an error in Nature,
the still point of the world, the link that won't hold,
the thread to untangle that will finally
lead to the heart of a truth.
The eye scans its surroundings,
the mind inquires aligns divides
in the perfume that diffuses
at the day's most languid.
It's in these silences you see
in every fleeting human
shadow some disturbed Divinity.

But the illusion fails, and time returns us
to noisy cities where the blue
is seen in patches, up between the roofs.
And the rain exhausts the earth;
winter's tedium weighs the houses down,
the light turns miserly – the soul bitter.
Till one day through a half-shut gate
in a courtyard, there among the trees,
we can see the yellow of the lemons;
and the chill in the heart
thaws, and deep in us
the golden horns of sunlight
pelt their songs.

EUGENIO MONTALE (1896 – 1981)
TRANSLATED BY JONATHAN GALASSI

NOT FOR EVERYBODY

Look where I reach
is only some can come –
not even plenty some.
Just few. Me, you
and who we say.

Ask any market woman
how tomato stay
when every Quaco
and him cousin
touch-touch it up.

How I did fool!
One mango
to one mouth
me say one time.

How I could
think good
fruit could be
for everybody?

STRAWBERRIES

There were never strawberries
like the ones we had
that sultry afternoon
sitting on the step
of the open french window
facing each other
your knees held in mine
the blue plates in our laps
the strawberries glistening
in the hot sunlight
we dipped them in sugar
looking at each other
not hurrying the feast
for one to come
the empty plates
laid on the stone together
with the two forks crossed
and I bent towards you
sweet in that air
in my arms
abandoned like a child
from your eager mouth
the taste of strawberries
in my memory
lean back again

let me love you
let the sun beat
on our forgetfulness
one hour of all
the heat intense
and summer lightning
on the Kilpatrick hills

let the storm wash the plates

AUGUST MORNING, UPPER BROADWAY

As the body of the beloved is a window
through which we behold the blackness and vastness
        of space
pulsing with stars, and as the man

on the corner with his fruit stand is a window,
and the cherries, blackberries, raspberries
avocados and carrots are a rose window

like the one in Chartres, yes, or the one in Paris
through which light floods from the other world, the
        pure one
stabbing tourists with malicious abundant joy

though the man is tired in the summer heat
and reads his newspaper listlessly, without passion
and people pass his stand buying nothing

let us call this scene a window looking out
not at a paradise but as a paradise
might be, if we had eyes to see

the women in their swaying dresses, the season's fruit
the babies in their strollers infinitely soft: clear window
after clear window

ALICIA SUSKIN OSTRIKER (1937 –)   79

AUBADE: SOME PEACHES, AFTER STORM

So that each
is its own, now – each a fallen, blond stillness.
Closer, above them,
the damselflies pass as they would over water,
if the fruit were water,
or as bees would, if they weren't
somewhere else, had the fruit found
already a point more steep
in rot, as soon it must, if
none shall lift it from the grass whose damp only
softens further those parts where flesh
goes soft.

There are those
whom no amount of patience looks likely
to improve ever, I always said, meaning
gift is random,
assigned here,
here withheld – almost always
correctly,
as it's turned out: how your hands clear
easily the wreckage;
how you stand – like a building for a time condemned,
then deemed historic. Yes. You
will be saved.

LESSON FROM THE ACADEMY

I throw this apple before you.
Take it — if you love me purely,
and give up your virginity.

Yet if you will not love me
keep the apple — and think
how long the beauty lasts.

PLATO (*c.* 427 − 348 BCE)
TRANSLATED BY WILLIS BARNSTONE

OF THE SENSUAL WORLD

Most beautiful of things I leave is sunlight;
then come glazing stars and the moon's face;
then ripe cucumbers and apples and pears.

FRUIT BOWL

A hand reaches toward the arrangement of fruit and, like a bee, hovers over it. The circle where the fingers glide is drawn tight as a trap – then they resume their flight, leaving at the bottom of the dish a bright red scar. A drop of blood, of honey, on the fingertips.

Between light and teeth, the web of desire weaves the bowlful of lips.

PIERRE REVERDY (1889–1960)
TRANSLATED BY DAN BELLM

THE FRUIT CARRIER

So this is what the year is.
Round as you are, you still are not heads:
you were thought of out there, O ripened fruit,
the winters imagined you, calculated you,
in the roots, under the bark of trunks
(in lamplight).
But still you are more beautiful
than all those plans, O you beloved works.
And I, I carry you. Your weight
makes me more serious than I am.
Despite myself, I betray some vague regret
like that of the astonished bride
as she starts to embrace,
one by one, her pale childhood friends.

84   RAINER MARIA RILKE (1875 – 1926)
TRANSLATED BY A. POULIN, JR.

THE APPLES OF THE HESPERIDES II

Such a lot of confusion, so many killings for nothing.
    The hero
of Tiryns took the golden apples to Euristheus. He
    gave them back.
Then *he* presented them to Athena. Then *she* returned
    them
to the Garden of the Hesperides – their source.
    Perhaps they meant in this way
to show how futile the Labours were, the endless
    circle – dull philosophies.
We, meanwhile, had come to imagine those apples
    gleaming
in a white bowl, on the wide, beautifully-set table
with an embroidered linen tablecloth, – at some Greek
    summer noon
when the unchangeable light streams through the
    windows and outside
the frantic cicadas are heard, and the swimmers down
    on the beach.
With something still left over: the two jars of Medeas
    and Achemoros.

YANNIS RITSOS (1909–90)   85
TRANSLATED BY GWENDOLYN MacEWEN and
NIKOS TSINGOS

From GOBLIN MARKET

Morning and evening
Maids heard the goblins cry:
"Come buy our orchard fruits,
Come buy, come buy:
Apples and quinces,
Lemons and oranges,
Plump unpeck'd cherries,
Melons and raspberries,
Bloom-down-cheek'd peaches,
Swart-headed mulberries,
Wild free-born cranberries,
Crab-apples, dewberries,
Pine-apples, blackberries,
Apricots, strawberries; –
All ripe together
In summer weather, –
Morns that pass by,
Fair eves that fly;
Come buy, come buy:
Our grapes fresh from the vine,
Pomegranates full and fine,
Dates and sharp bullaces,
Rare pears and greengages,
Damsons and bilberries,
Taste them and try:

Currants and gooseberries,
Bright-fire-like barberries,
Figs to fill your mouth,
Citrons from the South,
Sweet to tongue and sound to eye;
Come buy, come buy."

BALLAD OF ORANGE AND GRAPE

After you finish your work
after you do your day
after you've read your reading
after you've written your say —
you go down the street to the hot dog stand,
one block down and across the way.
On a blistering afternoon in East Harlem in the
        twentieth century.

Most of the windows are boarded up,
the rats run out of a sack —
sticking out of the crummy garage
one shiny long Cadillac;
at the glass door of the drug-addiction center,
a man who'd like to break your back.
But here's a brown woman with a little girl dressed in
        rose and pink, too.

Frankfurters frankfurters sizzle on the steel
where the hot-dog-man leans —
nothing else on the counter
but the usual two machines,
the grape one, empty, and the orange one, empty,
I face him in between.

A black boy comes along, looks at the hot dogs, goes
    on walking.

I watch the man as he stands and pours
in the familiar shape
bright purple in the one marked ORANGE
orange in the one marked GRAPE,
the grape drink in the machine marked ORANGE
and orange drink in the GRAPE.
Just the one word large and clear, unmistakable, on
    each machine.

I ask him: How can we go on reading
and make sense out of what we read? –
How can they write and believe what they're writing,
the young ones across the street,
while you go on pouring grape into ORANGE
and orange into the one marked GRAPE – ?
(How are we going to believe what we read and we
    write and we hear and we say and we do?)

He looks at the two machines and he smiles
and he shrugs and smiles and pours again.
It could be violence and nonviolence
it could be white and black   women and men
it could be war and peace or any
binary system, love and hate, enemy, friend.

Yes and no, be and not-be, what we do and what we
    don't do.

On a corner in East Harlem
garbage, reading, a deep smile, rape,
forgetfulness, a hot street of murder,
misery, withered hope,
a man keeps pouring grape into ORANGE
and orange into the one marked GRAPE,
pouring orange into GRAPE and grape into
    ORANGE forever.

THE VIRGIN

Like a sweet apple reddening on a high branch,
on the tip of the topmost branch and forgotten
by the apple pickers – no, beyond their reach.

Like a hyacinth in the mountains that shepherd men
trample down with their feet, and on the earth
the purple flower

SAPPHO (*c.* 630 – 570 BCE)

TRANSLATED BY WILLIS BARNSTONE

APPLES SWEETEN IN THE DARK

Growth is silent,
visible only after the event;
the infant's head
larger on the pillow
in the morning.

MY GRANDFATHER'S GARDEN

Where bloodshot apples peered from the grass
and seed packets taught me the patience
of waiting through a season.

Where I cracked the seams of pods,
and fired out peas with a thumbnail
pushed along the down of the soft inside.

Where he kept order with hoe prods
at the stems of lettuces, emerging like
overgrown moth-eaten flowers, colours drained.

Where I crouched on the shed's corrugate roof,
touching ripe damsons, which fell into the lap
of my stretched T-shirt.

Where I have come now, a month after his death,
the house and garden following him out of my life,
to cut back brambles and pack away tools.

Where, entering the hollow socket of the shed,
I hear damsons tap the roof,
telling me there is no one to catch them.

OWEN SHEERS (1974–)

THE STRAWBERRY PLANT

The rootless strawberry plant
Moves across the soil. It hops
Six inches. Has no single location,
Or root.
You cannot point to its origin,
Or parent. It shoots out
A pipe, and one more plant
Consolidates its ground.
It puts out crude petals, loosely met.
As if the business of flowering
Were to be got over. Their period is brief.
Even then, the fruit is green,
Swart, hairy. Its petals invite tearing
And are gone quickly,
As if they had been. The fruit swells,
Reddens, becomes succulent.
Propagation through the devouring
Appetite of another.
Is sweet, seeded, untruculent;
Slugs like it, all over.
It is nubile to the lips,
And survives even them. And teeth,
Insane with edible fury,
Of the loving kind.

WATERMELONS

Green Buddhas
On the fruit stand.
We eat the smile
And spit out the teeth.

ORANGES

The first time I walked
With a girl, I was twelve,
Cold, and weighted down
With two oranges in my jacket.
December. Frost cracking
Beneath my steps, my breath
Before me, then gone,
As I walked toward
Her house, the one whose
Porch light burned yellow
Night and day, in any weather.
A dog barked at me, until
She came out pulling
At her gloves, face bright
With rouge. I smiled,
Touched her shoulder, and led
Her down the street, across
A used car lot and a line
Of newly planted trees,
Until we were breathing
Before a drugstore. We
Entered, the tiny bell
Bringing a saleslady
Down a narrow aisle of goods.
I turned to the candies

Tiered like bleachers,
And asked what she wanted –
Light in her eyes, a smile
Starting at the corners
Of her mouth. I fingered
A nickel in my pocket,
And when she lifted a chocolate
That cost a dime,
I didn't say anything.
I took the nickel from
My pocket, then an orange,
And set them quietly on
The counter. When I looked up,
The lady's eyes met mine,
And held them, knowing
Very well what it was all
About.
      Outside,
A few cars hissing past,
Fog hanging like old
Coats between the trees.
I took my girl's hand
In mine for two blocks,
Then released it to let
Her unwrap the chocolate.
I peeled my orange
That was so bright against

The gray of December
That, from some distance,
Someone might have thought
I was making a fire in my hands.

"THE GARDEN WAS THICK . . ."

The garden was thick. Figs hung from their branches;
among the medlars poppies shouted summer.

Pruning and planting had been a heavy labor,
but now you heard God breathing on the fields.

The grapes were hugely swollen. Sweet, strong juice
dripped from the Flemish velvet of a peach.

Two love-struck butterflies proclaimed the ritual
festival of harvest, in San Giovanni al Monte.

Suddenly – breath of bad luck – I sensed the shadow
that stood out darkly on the grassy path.

I turned. And from the gate arose the figure
of the new gardener, who was hunting me.

MARIA LUISA SPAZIANI (1922–2014)
TRANSLATED BY GEOFFREY BROCK

THE STREET OF THE FRUIT STALLS

Wicks balance flame, a dark dew falls
in the street of the fruit stalls
melon, guava, mandarin
pyramid-piled like cannon balls,
glow red-hot, gold-hot, from within.

Dark children with a coin to spend
enter the lantern's orbit; find
melon, guava, mandarin –
the moon compacted to a rind,
the sun in a pitted skin

They take it, break it open, let
a gold or silver fountain wet
mouth, fingers, cheek, nose, chin;
radiant as lanterns, they forget
the dark street I am standing in.

RAISINS

Whose veins, whose loves, whose traces,
Whose time evaporated in the wrinkles of raisins.

The cool grains of past summers. You eat them and
      you eat.
As you would eat the fingertips of god, who holds all.

Reduced to the utter humility of the aged.
Like handfuls of pensioners on a religious trip.

They rise from the table and plunge into your roof.
The whole bunch rises. Truly rises.

Whose arteries, whose fears, whose traces,
Whose gargling you gulp down with the wrinkles of
      raisins.

The aged fingers grab you from within,
Choking you until you spit out their name.

ALEŠ ŠTEGER (1973–)   101
TRANSLATED BY BRIAN HENRY

A DISH OF PEACHES IN RUSSIA

With my whole body I taste these peaches,
I touch them and smell them. Who speaks?

I absorb them as the Angevine
Absorbs Anjou. I see them as a lover sees,

As a young lover sees the first buds of spring
And as the black Spaniard plays his guitar.

Who speaks? But it must be that I,
That animal, that Russian, that exile, for whom

The bells of the chapel pullulate sounds at
Heart. The peaches are large and round,

Ah! and red; and they have peach fuzz, ah!
They are full of juice and the skin is soft.

They are full of the colors of my village
And of fair weather, summer, dew, peace.

The room is quiet where they are.
The windows are open. The sunlight fills

The curtains. Even the drifting of the curtains,
Slight as it is, disturbs me. I did not know

That such ferocities could tear
One self from another, as these peaches do.

STONE FIG

The young fig tree feels with its hands
along the white sunny wall
and at the end of August
produces seven fruits,
seven royal fists that will be
runny with seed, ripe
with a musky honey that rarefies sweetness.

For the sick woman in the bedroom
behind the all-day-drawn curtains
I set the fruit in the sun
by the kitchen window.
Seven brimming wineskins
and a flint from the garden
she must have collected with a smile,
for it looks exactly like a fig.

A stone fig,
a hard, smooth, comfort-in-the-hand
Platonic Idea of Fig.
I watch the others daily for readiness;
this one, and now that one.

As if they were the last of her feelings
the old lady gobbles the figs.

Quickly, quickly, such greediness.
She eats them like anaesthetic.
Here's pith in her pale fingernails,
purple on the stubble of her chin.

Her legs are dry twigs. She can't
trust them to take her to the toilet,
then back again. Her skin is mottled
with overripeness I look away from.

She wants, she smiles, to sleep
and sleep and sleep. And then
to sleep again.

TABLEAU

At breakfast, the scent of lemons,
just-picked, yellowing on the sill.
At the table, a man and woman.

Between them, a still life:
shallow bowl, damask plums
in one square of morning light.

The woman sips tea
from a chipped blue cup, turning it,
avoiding the rough white edge.

The man, his thumb pushing deep
toward the pit, peels taut skin
clean from plum flesh.

The woman watches his hands,
the pale fruit darkening
wherever he's pushed too hard.

She is thinking *seed*, the hardness
she'll roll on her tongue,
a beginning. One by one,

the man fills the bowl with globes
that glisten. *Translucent*, he thinks.
The woman, now, her cup tilting

empty, sees, for the first time,
the hairline crack
that has begun to split the bowl in half.

POMEGRANATES

Thick-skinned pomegranates, your rinds
forced open by a rashness of seeds, you've led
me to envisage the highest foreheads
bursting with all that comes to mind.

Should all those suns you suffer,
O pomegranates with gaping sides,
leave you so swollen with pride
as to break down your ruby buffers,

should the wizened gold of your skin
give way to pressure from within
and explode in red juice-gems,

that light-shedding fracture
might bring a soul such as I had to dream
of its own hidden architecture.

108   PAUL VALÉRY (1871–1945)
      TRANSLATED BY PAUL MULDOON

MY ORANGE

Take one
from the basket
with the cup of bittersweet coffee, this is all
I'm going to get this morning because
Vittorini is teaching me again another membrane

of truth so do not repeat
my spendthrift days, the ones that went
uneaten, little suns on my bookshelf
dried up pulp and laces.
Now when I try for greater focus
every plate means something and yes there's no
food in *The Charterhouse of Parma* because Stendhal
        was obese,
maybe punishing himself, now there's another
        new war
and time is so tight. Now bend my thumb

angle it down through the oily skin
of the globe, thank
the old cast-offs
tucked into the toes of the Christmas stockings
(I was digging for Kennedy halves
and the walnuts and chocolates). In the lunch box
I wanted concentrate

or the horrible Tang
the astronauts packed into space – Though we're
    known
throughout the world
for our bombs,
our baskets glow with the light
of a thousand miles of trees
and the human
fingers of the pickers
burnt with the sweet acid.

From THE TRIANGULAR PEAR

Prelude I

Be discovered, America!
Eureka!

I measure, explore,
                    discover, all out of breath,

In America, *America,*
In myself, *myself.*

I peel the skin from the planet,
                    sweep away mold and dust;
Cut through the crust
                    and go down
                                into the depths of things
As into the subway.

Down there grow triangular pears;
                    I seek the naked souls they contain.

I take the trapezoidal fruit, not to eat
Of it; but to let its glassy core
Glow with an altar's red heat.

Pry into it incessantly,
                    do not relent;
Do not be misled
If they say your watermelon's green when in fact
    it's red.
I worry it like a retriever,
                    hack at it like a cleaver!
And if the poet's a hooligan,
Then so was Columbus – carry on!

Follow your mad bent –
                    head straight for shore . . .
You're looking for India –
                    look a bit more –

You'll find
        America!

TRANSLATED BY WILLIAM JAY SMITH

STRAWBERRIES

When you come to sleep with me
wear a black dress
printed with strawberries
and a black top hat
decorated with strawberries
and hold a basket of strawberries
and sell me strawberries
tell me in a sweet light voice
strawberries strawberries
who wants strawberries
don't wear anything under the dress
afterwards
strings will lift you up
invisible or visible
and lower you
directly on my prick.

YONA WALLACH (1944–85)
TRANSLATED BY LINDA STERN ZISQUIT

THIS IS JUST TO SAY

I have eaten
the plums
that were in
the icebox

and which
you were probably
saving
for breakfast

Forgive me
they were delicious
so sweet
and so cold

VEGETABLES

ASPARAGUS

Minnows of the air, swallows
and later bats, untatting the garden's
lace of gnats and mosquitoes, and at
the garden's edge the fungi, smoke
and ink, fringe-gilled, raw-capped, ragged
and still in veil, the havishammed,
unlike ourselves, not bud, not born,
not bridal but spores, a net drifting
down to rest on everything, spade
and fork and glove, before the flower
bursts its stem, the rush of green *how I
love how I hate this place we've made*

KAREN LEONA ANDERSON (1973−)

From INANNA: QUEEN OF HEAVEN
AND EARTH

Inanna sang:
He has sprouted; he has burgeoned;
He is lettuce planted by the water.
He is the one my womb loves best.

My well-stocked garden of the plain,
My barley growing high in its furrow,
My apple tree which bears fruit up to its crown,
He is lettuce planted by the water.

My honey-man, my honey-man sweetens me always.
My lord, the honey-man of the gods,
He is the one my womb loves best.
His hand is honey, his foot is honey,
He sweetens me always.

My eager impetuous caresser of the navel,
My caresser of the soft thighs,
He is the one my womb loves best,
He is lettuce planted by the water.

ANONYMOUS (*c.* 2000 BCE)
VERSION BY DIANE WOLKSTEIN and
SAMUEL NOAH KRAMER

From THE EXETER BOOK

A Riddle

I am a wondrous creature, a joy to women,
a help to neighbours; I harm none
of the city-dwellers, except for my killer.
My base is steep and high, I stand in a bed,
shaggy somewhere beneath. Sometimes ventures
the very beautiful daughter of a churl,
a maid proud in mind, so that she grabs hold of me,
rubs me to redness, ravages my head,
forces me into a fastness. Immediately she feels
my meeting, the one who confines me,
the curly-locked woman. Wet will be that eye.

⌈onion⌉

ANONYMOUS (10TH CENTURY)   119
TRANSLATED BY MEGAN CAVELL

ZUCCHINI

My grandmother cored them
with a serrated knife

with her hands that had come
through the slaughter –

So many hours I stared at the blotch
marks on her knuckles,

her strong fingers around the
long green gourd –

In a glass bowl the stuffing was setting –
chopped lamb, tomato pulp, raw rice, lemon juice,

a sand brew of spices –
from the riverbank of her birth –

Can holding on to this image
help me make sense of time?

the temporal waves,
waves smashing and lipping

the pulverized stone; a bird dissolving
into a cloud bank in late day;

the happy and sad steps we walked

along the plaster walls and steel bridges,
the glass façades, highways of glistening money

the objects we caress in dreams
from which we wake to find the hallway dark,

the small light at the bottom of the stairs,
the kitchen waiting with a scent

of zucchini sautéed in olive oil
onions and oregano,

a waft of last night's red wine – a gulp
of cold water to bring on the day.

GARLIC

The back door faces north. The pail I left

in the rain has formed a hoop of dirty ice,

dry and hard as iron. The air's a vice

that clamps the ribs and almost stops the breath.

I'm planting garlic. Soil, forked over only

yesterday, is rigid now; the spade strikes

and sings aloud, as though I had hit stone.

With cold red fingers I tamp in the moonlike

cloves, carefully set them in fresh compost

from my heap, which, even in this freezing

season, is warm and sweet. I chop with my trowel

at lumps, trying to form a tilth; kneeling

in white rime I imagine summer's tossed

lettuce, endives, capers, vinegar, olive oil.

122   GERARD BENSON (1931–2014)

CABBAGE AND CARROT

One afternoon Cabbage visited Carrot
and found Carrot wearing something transparent.

"Oh, that looks quite fancy, that looks like fun.
But where are you off to in this cellophane?"

"You really think so?" blushed Carrot. "Well, I've . . .
Well, I've been invited tonight by the Knife.

"And I've been invited – please, don't get me wrong –
alone. I don't think I can bring you along."

"The Knife!" Cabbage shouted, disgusted. "Big deal!
Who cares for that cheap imitation of steel?

"I'm going out tonight, too, without you.
Two Spoons have invited myself for a stew."

JOSEPH BRODSKY (1940–96)

SPRAYING THE POTATOES

Knapsack-sprayer on my back, I marched the drills
Of blossoming potatoes – Kerr's Pinks in a frivelled
    blue,
The Arran Banners wearing white. July was due,
A haze of copper sulphate on the far-off hills.

The bronze noon air was drowsy, unguent as glue.
As I bent over the big oil-drum for a refill
I heard the axle-roll of a rut-locked tumbril.
It might have come from God-knows-where, or out
    of the blue.

A verdant man was cuffed and shackled to its bed.
Fourteen troopers rode beside, all dressed in red.
It took them a minute to string him up from the
    oak tree.

I watched him swing in his Derry green for hours
    and hours,
His popping eyes of apoplectic liberty
That blindly scanned the blue and white potato
    flowers.

"IUVENTIUS, WERE I ALLOWED ..."

Iuventius,
were I allowed
to kiss your eyes
as sweet as honey
on & on, three
thousand kisses
would not seem
too much for me,
as many as
ripe harvest ears
of sheaves of corn
would still not be
too much of kiss-
ing you, for me.

CATULLUS (*c.* 84–54 BCE)

TRANSLATED BY PETER WHIGHAM

CUTTING GREENS

curling them around
i hold their bodies in obscene embrace
thinking of everything but kinship.
collards and kale
strain against each strange other
away from my kissmaking hand and
the iron bedpot.
the pot is black,
the cutting board is black,
my hand,
and just for a minute
the greens roll black under the knife,
and the kitchen twists dark on its spine
and i taste in my natural appetite
the bond of live things everywhere.

LETTUCE

Some think your commendation you deserve,
'Cause you of old *Augustus* did preserve.
Why did you still prolong that fatal breath,
That banish'd *Ovid*, and was *Tully*'s death?
But I suppose that neither of 'em you,
Nor Orator nor Poet ever knew;
Wherefore I wonder not, you shou'd comply,
And the Worlds Tyrant so far gratify.
Thou truly to all Tyrants art of use,
Their madness flies before thy pow'rful juice.
Their heads with better wreaths, I pri'thee, crown,
And let the World in them thy kindness own.
At thy command forth from its scorched Heart,
Of Tyrants Love the greatest does depart.
False Love, I mean; for thou ne'r try'st t'expel
True Love, who, like a good King, governs well.
Justly that Dog star, *Cupid*, thou do'st hate,
Whose fire kills Herbs, and Monsters does create.

[*Augustus* is said to have been preserved in his Sickness by
    Lettuce. Plin.]

ABRAHAM COWLEY (1618–67)   127

From THE BOTANIC GARDEN

SYLPHS! as you hover on ethereal wing,
Brood the green children of parturient Spring! —
Where in their bursting cells my Embryons rest,
I charge you guard the vegetable nest;
Count with nice eye the myriad SEEDS, that swell
Each vaulted womb of husk, or pod, or shell;
Feed with sweet juices, clothe with downy hair,
Or hang, inshrined, their little orbs in air.

SPINACH

This beautiful spinach hasn't once
hidden you in its green shirt.
You have never worn
any green shirts at all.
You avoid this kind of image –
yet I can clearly remember
your silent flesh resembled
a seed at its apex.
Why does spinach look
beautiful? Why
do I know you will think
this question, but won't ask it?
Washing spinach, I feel
its deep green quality
is like a child I had with the plant.
So spinach answers the question
of how we can see in our lives
angels that others say don't exist.
The beauty of spinach is weak –
when we face the mere fifty square meters
of standard living space, this vivid spinach
is the weakest politics. On the surface
a bit wild, difficult to clean –

its beauty one might say
is sustained by the power of little irritations.
Yet its nourishment determines
its value, not to the left nor to the right.

ZANG DI (1964–)
TRANSLATED BY ELEANOR GOODMAN and
AO WANG

"FORBIDDEN FRUIT A FLAVOR HAS"

Forbidden Fruit a flavor has
That lawful Orchards mocks –
How luscious lies within the Pod
The Pea that Duty locks –

TOMATOES

A woman travels to Brazil for plastic
surgery and a face-lift. She is sixty
and has the usual desire to stay pretty.
Once she is healed, she takes her new face
out on the streets of Rio. A young man
with a gun wants her money. Bang, she's dead.
The body is shipped back to New York,
but in the morgue there is a mix-up. The son
is sent for. He is told that his mother
is one of these ten different women.
Each has been shot. Such is modern life.
He studies them all but can't find her.
With her new face, she has become a stranger.
Maybe it's this one, maybe it's that one.
He looks at their breasts. Which ones nursed him?
He presses their hands to his cheek.
Which ones consoled him? He even tries
climbing into their laps to see which
feels most familiar but the coroner stops him.
Well, says the coroner, which is your mother?
They all are, says the young man, let me
take them as a package. The coroner hesitates,
then agrees. Actually, it solved a lot of problems.
The young man has the ten women shipped home,
then cremates them all together. You've seen

how some people have a little urn on the mantel?
This man has a huge silver garbage can.
In the spring, he drags the garbage can
out to the garden and begins working the teeth,
the ash, the bits of bone into the soil.
Then he plants tomatoes. His mother loved tomatoes.
They grow straight from seed, so fast and big
that the young man is amazed. He takes the first
ten into the kitchen. In their roundness,
he sees his mother's breasts. In their smoothness,
he finds the consoling touch of her hands.
Mother, mother, he cries, and flings himself
on the tomatoes. Forget about the knife, the fork,
the pinch of salt. Try to imagine the filial
starvation, think of his ravenous kisses.

From POLY-OLBION

The Cole-wort, Cauliflower, and Cabbage, in
    their season,
The Rouncefall, great beans, and early ripening
    peason:
The Onion, Scallion, Leek, which housewives
    highly rate;
Their kinsmen Garlic then, the poor man's
    Mithridate;
The savoury Parsnip next, and Carrot pleasing food;
The Skirret (which some way) in sallats stirs
    the blood;
The Turnip, tasting well to clowns in winter weather.
Thus in our verse we pott, roots, herbs, and fruits
    together.
The great moist Pumpkin (pumpion) then that on the
    ground doth lie,
A purer of his kind, the sweet Muskmullion by;
Which dainty palates now, because they would
    not want,
Have kindly learned to set, as yearly to transplant.

FIELD OF LETTUCE

So much of the row today is given to the ubiquitous
green of iceberg, whose empty head so easily rolls
from bed to simple wrapping,

or the coarser leaves with a history of romaine
in their spines, a bitter output even hares may reject.

So much is tasteless, cold, even Boston, set apart,

overproduced, a species unto itself, so pure (blandly
incestuous) a leaf only the gourmand can taste it.

But *Min* demanded *Lactuca sativa*, a labial vessel –
Min, holding his cock and flail, in right hand and left,
Min, who drank the milk of the lettuce so he could
in turn provide the milk of the Nile, ached for the
    prickly

variant, the untamed leaf seeding wild among the
    tamed. O Black
God of Desire, demand again your portion, open
    this field,
make it give to you what was always yours to have.

POEM WITH A CUCUMBER IN IT

Sometimes from this hillside just after sunset
The rim of the sky takes on a tinge
Of the palest green, like the flesh of a cucumber
When you peel it carefully.

*

In Crete once, in the summer,
When it was still hot at midnight,
We sat in a taverna by the water
Watching the squid boats rocking in the moonlight,
Drinking retsina and eating salads
Of cool, chopped cucumber and yogurt and a
     little dill.

*

A hint of salt, something like starch, something
Like an attar of grasses or green leaves
On the tongue is the tongue
And the cucumber
Evolving toward each other.

*

Since *cumbersome* is a word,
Cumber must have been a word,
Lost to us now, and even then,
For a person feeling encumbered,
It must have felt orderly and right-minded
To stand at a sink and slice a cucumber.

*

If you think I am going to make
A sexual joke in this poem, you are mistaken.

*

In the old torment of the earth
When the fires were cooling and disposing themselves
Into granite and limestone and serpentine and shale,
It is possible to imagine that, under yellowish
    chemical clouds,
The molten froth, having burned long enough,
Was already dreaming of release,
And that the dream, dimly
But with increasingly distinctness, took the form
Of water, and that it was then, still more dimly, that it
    imagined
The dark green skin and opal green flesh of
    cucumbers.

ROBERT HASS (1941 −)   137

THE CUCUMBER
to Ekber Babayev

The snow is knee-deep in the courtyard
and still coming down hard:
it hasn't let up all morning.
We're in the kitchen.
On the table, on the oilcloth, spring –
on the table there's a very tender young cucumber,
                              pebbly and fresh as a daisy.
We're sitting around the table staring at it.
It softly lights up our faces,
and the very air smells fresh.
We're sitting around the table staring at it,
amazed
            thoughtful
                              optimistic.
We're as if in a dream.
On the table, on the oilcloth, hope –
on the table, beautiful days,
a cloud seeded with a green sun,
an emerald crowd impatient and on its way,
loves blooming openly –
on the table, there on the oilcloth, a very tender young
                                                    cucumber,
                              pebbly and fresh as a daisy.

The snow is knee-deep in the courtyard
and coming down hard.
It hasn't let up all morning.

NAZIM HIKMET (1902−63)

TRANSLATED BY RANDY BLASING and
MUTLU KONUK

"THE MAN PULLING RADISHES"

The man pulling radishes
Pointed the way
With a radish.

1942

The tomatoes are holding an emergency meeting.
Item one on the agenda: a Jewish boy keeps
appearing in their midst.
(When the Germans march past
my father practices being a very small potato.)

My father keeps appearing in their midst
because God
is not in Odesa in 1942
but the tomatoes are there, doing His work —

Inside each tomato, a boy finds
a new congregation: round rabbis, red as revelation,
        shield him
with their flesh. Outside, Hitler's mustache zigzags
        like a blackbird.
My father practices being a very small potato.

Abraham bargains with God at the vegetable market:
"What if I move this yellow tomato
to block Your view of certain fugitive children?"
But God is not in the market in 1942

when soldiers prod each crate and don't find the boy:
"Ve are just regular tomatoes.
Nothing to see here,"
(their papers are always in order).

In the history of fruit,
this moment is a chapter:
How tomatoes learned to smuggle children.
(My father perfected the art of being a very small
        potato.)

SPRAYING THE POTATOES

The barrels of blue potato-spray
Stood on a headland of July
Beside an orchard wall where roses
Were young girls hanging from the sky.

The flocks of green potato-stalks
Were blossom spread for sudden flight,
The Kerr's Pinks in a frivelled blue,
The Arran Banners wearing white.

And over that potato-field
A lazy veil of woven sun.
Dandelions growing on headlands, showing
Their unloved hearts to everyone.

And I was there with the knapsack sprayer
On the barrel's edge poised. A wasp was floating
Dead on a sunken briar leaf
Over a copper-poisoned ocean.

The axle-roll of a rut-locked cart
Broke the burnt stick of noon in two.
An old man came through a cornfield
Remembering his youth and some Ruth he knew.

He turned my way. "God further the work."
He echoed an ancient farming prayer.
I thanked him. He eyed the potato-drills.
He said: "You are bound to have good ones there."

We talked and our talk was a theme of kings,
A theme for strings. He hunkered down
In the shade of the orchard wall. O roses
The old man dies in the young girl's frown.

And poet lost to potato-fields,
Remembering the lime and copper smell
Of the spraying barrels he is not lost
Or till blossomed stalks cannot weave a spell.

MONOLOGUE FOR AN ONION

I don't mean to make you cry.
I mean nothing, but this has not kept you
From peeling away my body, layer by layer,

The tears clouding your eyes as the table fills
With husks, cut flesh, all the debris of pursuit.
Poor deluded human: you seek my heart.

Hunt all you want. Beneath each skin of mine
Lies another skin: I am pure onion – pure union
Of outside and in, surface and secret core.

Look at you, chopping and weeping. Idiot.
Is this the way you go through life, your mind
A stopless knife, driven by your fantasy of truth,

Of lasting union – slashing away skin after skin
From things, ruin and tears your only signs
Of progress? Enough is enough.

You must not grieve that the world is glimpsed
Through veils. How else can it be seen?
How will you rip away the veil of the eye, the veil

That you are, you who want to grasp the heart
Of things, hungry to know where meaning
Lies. Taste what you hold in your hands: onion-juice,

Yellow peels, my stinging shreds. You are the one
In pieces. Whatever you meant to love, in meaning to
You changed yourself: you are not who you are,

Your soul cut moment to moment by a blade
Of fresh desire, the ground sown with abandoned
     skins.
And at your inmost circle, what? A core that is

Not one. Poor fool, you are divided at the heart,
Lost in its maze of chambers, blood, and love,
A heart that will one day beat you to death.

146   SUJI KWOCK KIM (1969−)

THE SIMPLE TRUTH

I bought a dollar and a half's worth of small red
        potatoes,
took them home, boiled them in their jackets
and ate them for dinner with a little butter and salt.
Then I walked through the dried fields
on the edge of town. In middle June the light
hung on in the dark furrows at my feet,
and in the mountain oaks overhead the birds
were gathering for the night, the jays and mockers
squawking back and forth, the finches still darting
into the dusty light. The woman who sold me
the potatoes was from Poland; she was someone
out of my childhood in a pink spangled sweater and
        sunglasses
praising the perfection of all her fruits and vegetables
at the road-side stand and urging me to taste
even the pale, raw sweet corn trucked all the way,
she swore, from New Jersey. "Eat, eat," she said,
"Even if you don't I'll say you did."

                                Some things
you know all your life. They are so simple and true
they must be said without elegance, meter and rhyme,
they must be laid on the table beside the salt shaker,
the glass of water, the absence of light gathering
in the shadows of picture frames, they must be

naked and alone, they must stand for themselves.
My friend Henri and I arrived at this together in 1965
before I went away, before he began to kill himself,
and the two of us to betray our love. Can you taste
what I'm saying? It is onions or potatoes, a pinch
of simple salt, the wealth of melting butter, it is
     obvious,
it stays in the back of your throat like a truth
you never uttered because the time was always wrong,
it stays there for the rest of your life, unspoken,
made of that dirt we call earth, the metal we call salt,
in a form we have no words for, and you live on it.

CUCKOO CORN

The seed that goes into the ground
After the first cuckoo
Is said to grow short and light
As the beard of a boy.

Though Spring was slow this year
And the seed late,
After that Summer the corn was long
And heavy as the hair of any girl.

They claimed that she had no errand
Near the thresher,
This girl whose hair floated as if underwater
In a wind that would have cleaned corn,

Who was strangled by the flapping belt.
But she had reason,
I being her lover, she being that man's daughter,
Knowing of cuckoo corn, of seed and season.

PAUL MULDOON (1951 –)   149

ODE TO THE ARTICHOKE

The tender-hearted
artichoke
got dressed as a warrior,
erect, built
a little cupola,
stood
impermeable
under
its scales,
around it
the crazy vegetables
bristled,
grew
astonishing tendrils,
cattails, bulbs,
in the subsoil
slept the carrot
with its red whiskers,
the grapevine
dried the runners
through which it carries the wine,
the cabbage
devoted itself
to trying on skirts,
oregano

to perfuming the world,
and the gentle
artichoke
stood there in the garden,
dressed as a warrior,
burnished
like a pomegranate,
proud,
and one day
along with the others
in large willow
baskets, it traveled
to the market
to realize its dream:
the army.
Amid the rows
never was it so military
as at the fair,
men
among the vegetables
with their white shirts
were
marshals
of the artichokes,
the tight ranks,
the voices of command,
and the detonation

of a falling crate,
but
then
comes
Maria
with her basket,
picks
an artichoke,
isn't afraid of it,
examines it, holds it
to the light as if it were an egg,
buys it,
mixes it up
in her bag
with a pair of shoes,
with a head of cabbage and a
bottle
of vinegar
until
entering the kitchen
she submerges it in a pot.
Thus ends
in peace
the career
of the armored vegetable
which is called artichoke,
then

scale by scale
we undress
its delight
and we eat
the peaceful flesh
of its green heart.

PABLO NERUDA (1904—73)
TRANSLATED BY STEPHEN MITCHELL

IN THE POTATOES

Early Scots refused to eat (it was not
mentioned in the Bible): leprosy, blindness –
its supposed costly price. *"One potato,*
two potato, three potato, four!"
Misunderstood too: Captain Cook,
Walter Raleigh, even Catherine the Great

tried to convince people of the glorious crop
but failed. Lord Byron lamented its aphrodisiac effects
. . . *'Tis after all a sad result of passions and potatoes.*
The Quencha Indians of Peru have over one thousand
words for this crop. They dance a two-step during
        harvest,
pant legs rolled to knees, every jump a push of water

from the bitter, marble-sized tubers to make *chuno*
        paste.
In the blackfrost night, it dries, feeds a whole village
for two seasons: crystal starch. Potato spirits
made of rock line up in threes, hum soil-songs
through rooftops into ears of sleeping infants.
Estar en las papas – to be in the potatoes –

means a person has finally risen to afford more
than a banana diet. In the Paucartambo Valley
of Peru, I read the soft earth like Braille, gather
some on my own, each hardness a possibility.
Tiny pineapples, coral snakes, purple gumdrops —
anything but the brown oval spud I know. A small,
    flat one:

mishipasinghan — means cat's nose; a knobby,
difficult-to-peel kind is *lumchipamundana* — or, *potato
makes young bride weep*. The Acumbo village
sees a surplus of this kind in late summer.
Housewives grind their teeth with each peel,
stifle shivers into aprons, curse the abundant fruit.

THE POTATO-GATHERERS
(*on the painting by George Russell, AE*)

They know what they're doing at the worst of times,
these three unpraying desperadoes
on home ground. No time to notice
the sun's orange angelus at their backs,
any more than we, halfway back to them,
used to pause for the grey shine in October skies
as the digger clattered past, anointing us
with wormly wet earth and withered-white
potato-plant pipes as we clutched for the seed,
for cold gold in the seam of gutter.
In that impressionist twilight, you can't make out
their fingers; even their bent backs you'd see better
with our millennial 20-20 sight
from a west-bound jet over Belmullet.

NOT MY BUSINESS

They picked Akanni up one morning
Beat him soft like clay
And stuffed him down the belly
Of a waiting jeep.
What business of mine is it
So long they don't take the yam
From my savouring mouth?

They came one night
Booted the whole house awake
And dragged Danladi out,
Then off to a lengthy absence.
What business of mine is it
So long they don't take the yam
From my savouring mouth?

Chinwe went to work one day
Only to find her job was gone:
No query, no warning, no probe –
Just one neat sack for a stainless record.
What business of mine is it
So long they don't take the yam
From my savouring mouth?

And then one evening
As I sat down to eat my yam
A knock on the door froze my hungry hand.
The jeep was waiting on my bewildered lawn
Waiting, waiting in its usual silence.

CLEANING VEGETABLES

Sometimes the beet cries clearly
between the point of the knife
sunk in and the cool matter
of heart coaxed out.
Old skins like leaf-fall
pile in wet twists in the sink.

Maybe in sleep one hand washes the other;
otherwise too much imagining
would hold us off absurdly. For today,
cleaning the vegetables, I saw that
the small work grew large, brought
from random to a parable of waking.

And then another thing occurred to me
as I cut: the water took with it
the memories of other lives, the beards
of radishes and the black turnip
soils to a corner in the dark
where they couldn't get back.

Though it was possible to guess
the outcome of the disheveled mess
of bruised and roughened vegetable skins,
yet now the water meant clarity more

159

strongly than I'd imagined and made off
with those gathering flecks.

The feelings of misgiving flowed away
at once as the water and knife
made things especially clean. The potato
left its mealy skin, the lettuce became white,
the carrot gave up its fingerprint,
the avocado, its wooden heart.

ASPARAGUS

Pushing up, hard and fibrous
from the ground, it is said to be
grown for the mouth:
steamed till supple
so the stem is still firm
but with a slight give to gravity.

Each wand has spurs
that swell in bedded layers
to the dark tip – slubbed and imbricate,
tight-set and over-lapping round the bud.
In a slather and slide, butter
floods at the bulb-head.

ROBIN ROBERTSON (1955 –)

QUINCE, CABBAGE, MELON, AND CUCUMBER

Anything can be a marionette. A quince, a cabbage, a
    melon, a cucumber,
suspended against a black background, illumined by a
    curious
white light. In this little show, the quince plays a full
    gold moon. The cabbage
is the antagonist, curled outer leaves fingering the
    charcoal void.
Cucumber's the peasant, nubby belly to the ground
    like a frog.
That leaves melon, center stage, rough wedge hacked
    out of her buttery side.
Each object holds its space, drawing the eye from
    quince to cabbage, melon
to cucumber, in a left to right, downward-sloping
    curve. Four bodies
hang in the box of darkness like planets, each in its
    private orbit.
It's a quiet drama about nothing at all. No touch, no
    brushing
up against each other, no oxygen, no rot, so that each
    shape, each
character, is pure, clean in its loyalty to its own fierce
    standard.

Even the wounded melon exudes serenity. Somewhere,
  juice runs
down a hairy chin, but that is well beyond the border
  of the box.

From A MIDSUMMER NIGHT'S DREAM

So we grow together,
Like to a double cherry, seeming parted,
But yet an union in partition;
Two lovely berries moulded on one stem;
So, with two seeming bodies, but one heart.

Act III, Scene 2

And, most dear actors, eat no onions
Nor garlic, for we are to utter sweet breath;
And I do not doubt but to hear them say,
It is a sweet comedy.

Act IV, Scene 2

EAT

My mother is holding my infant son
so I can eat the mustard cabbage
she has sweetened with brown sugar.
For the starving children in China,
I have learned to eat whatever I am given.
Even mustard cabbage, which I hate.
She nods approvingly.
Now I must eat to feed
not only all the world's starving children
but my own flesh and blood,
my infant son
who fattens daily on my milk,
my milk that trickles a thin blue stream
into his wet pink mouth.

I grow thinner.

He is sucking the living
daylights out of you,
says my mother,
and with a bamboo rice stick paddle,
she slaps another helping onto my plate.

PRAYER FOR AN INMATE OF RVJDC

God is probably a Belgian endive,
which is a vegetable I don't believe in.

A fist-sized, tender, lettuce-looking thing
that sprouts from chicory, under covering

of dust and darkness. If it's lopped from the root,
another grows and grows, until some rot

takes hold. That's the point, most likely,
when someone cleans and grinds the chicory

to make the coffee you're drinking, which looks
almost good – thick as ink on a handmade book –

but lots of things appear as what they're not.
Once you've snapped the endive's huddled

leaves from their whiskered base, there's no hiding
the kind of bitterness you've got.

166   D. M. SPRATLEY (1986 –)

VEGETABLES I

In the vegetable department
The eggplants lay in bruised disorder;
Gleaming, almost black,
Their skins oiled and bitter;
A mutilated stem twisting
From each swollen purple body
Where it had hung pendulous
From the parent.
They were almost the size
Of human heads, decapitated.
A fingernail tearing the skin
Disclosed pith, green-white,
Utterly drained of blood.
Inside each skull, pulp;
Close packed, dry and coarse.
As though the fontanels
Had ossified too soon.
Some of these seemed to be smiling
In a shy embarrassed manner,
Jostling among themselves.

WHEN I AM DIGGING POTATOES

I am digging potatoes for dinner,
an ant climbs my naked leg.
– Ant, what do you think
of eternity?

The ant has a superhuman face
like chemical processes
in the sun.
The ant can educate me
in questions of eternity.

Digging potatoes
improves the mind.

168   ANNA SWIR (1909–84)
TRANSLATED BY CZESŁAW MIŁOSZ and
LEONARD NATHAN

THE ONION

The onion, now that's something else.
Its innards don't exist.
Nothing but pure onionhood
fills this devout onionist.
Oniony on the inside,
onionesque it appears.
It follows its own daimonion
without our human tears.

Our skin is just a cover-up
for the land where none dare go,
an internal inferno,
the anathema of anatomy.
In an onion there's only onion
from its top to its toe,
onionymous monomania,
unanimous omninudity.

At peace, of a piece,
internally at rest.
Inside it, there's a smaller one
of undiminished worth.
The second holds a third one,
the third contains a fourth.

A centripetal fugue.
Polyphony compressed.

Nature's rotundest tummy,
its greatest success story,
the onion drapes itself in its
own aureoles of glory.
We hold veins, nerves, and fat,
secretions' secret sections.
Not for us such idiotic
onionoid perfections.

170   WISŁAWA SZYMBORSKA (1923–2012)
TRANSLATED BY STANISŁAW BARAŃCZAK and
CLARE CAVANAGH

DIGGING

To-day I think
Only with scents, – scents dead leaves yield,
And bracken, and wild carrot's seed,
And the square mustard field;

Odours that rise
When the spade wounds the root of tree,
Rose, currant, raspberry, or goutweed,
Rhubarb or celery;

The smoke's smell, too,
Flowing from where a bonfire burns
The dead, the waste, the dangerous,
And all to sweetness turns.

It is enough
To smell, to crumble the dark earth,
While the robin sings over again
Sad songs of Autumn mirth.

EDWARD THOMAS (1878 – 1917)

MATACHE MARKET SEEN FROM BOSTON

In the tiny gardens on Commonwealth Avenue
some crocuses and daffodils sprout next to snow piles,
and so does the strutting blue-purple cabbage
treated here, in America, as ornamental plant
resembling a young ballerina
sheathed in translucent tulle.

How distant she keeps herself from her sister in the
        Matache Market:
greenish pale, perfect for the poor's favorite dishes
or for pickling over winter.

"Sour cabbage, wide-leafed, sour cabbage
for *sarmale*," calls out the auntie from Bucovina,
queen of barrels brimming with pickled cabbage.

172 LILIANA URSU (1949–)
        TRANSLATED BY MIHAELA MOSCALIUC

THE CORN BABY

They brought it. It was brought
from the field, the last sheaf, the last bundle

the latest and most final armful. Up up
over the head, hold it, hold it high, it held

the gazer's gaze, it held hope, did hold it.
Through the stubble of September, on shoulders

aloft, hardly anything, it weighed, like a sparrow,
it was said, something winged, hollow, though

pulsing, freed from the field
where it flailed in wind, where it waited, wanted

to be found and bound with cord. It had
limbs, it had legs. And hands. It had fingers.

Fingers and a face peering from the stalks,
shuttered in the grain, closed, though just a kernel,

a shut corn. They brought him and autumn
rushed in, tossed its cape of starlings,

tattered the frost-spackled field.

MARK WUNDERLICH (1968–) 173

SPICES, HERBS, LEGUMES, etc.

THE LAST SAFFRON
for Vidur Wazir

*Next to saffron cultivation in interest come the floating
gardens of the Dal Lake that can be towed from place
to place.*

1

I will die, in autumn, in Kashmir,
and the shadowed routine of each vein
will almost be news, the blood censored,
for the *Saffron Sun* and the *Times of Rain*

will be sold in black, then destroyed,
invisibly at Zero Taxi Stand.
There will be men nailing tabloids
to the fence of Grindlay's Bank,

I will look for any sign of blood
in captions under the photos of boys,
those who by inches – after the April flood –
were killed in fluted waters, each voice

torn from its throat as the Jhelum
receded to their accounts and found cash

sealed in the bank's reflection.
I will open the waves, draw each hushed

balance, ready to pay, by any means,
whatever the drivers ask. The one
called *Eyes of Maple Green*
will promise, "I'll take you anywhere, even

in curfew hours," and give me a bouquet –
"There's a ban on wreaths!"

2

    I will die that day in late October, it will be long ago:

    He will take me to Pampore where I'll gather flowers
and run back to the taxi, stamens – How many thou-
sands? – crushed to red varnish in my hands: I'll shout:
"Saffron, my payment!" And he'll break the limits,
chase each rumor of me. "No one's seen Shahid," we'll
hear again and again, in every tea house from Nishat
to Naseem. He will stop by the Shalimar *ghats*, and
we'll descend the steps to the water. He'll sever some
land – two yards – from the shore, I, his last passenger.
Suddenly he'll age, his voice will break, his gaze green
water, washing me: "It won't grow again, this gold

from the burned fields of Pampore." And he will row
the freed earth past the Security zones, so my blood is
news in the *Saffron Sun* setting on the waves.

3

       Yes, I remember it,
the day I'll die, I broadcast the crimson,

so long ago of that sky, its spread air,
its rushing dyes, and a piece of earth

bleeding, apart from the shore, as we went
on the day I'll die, past the guards, and he,

keeper of the world's last saffron, rowed me
on an island the size of a grave. On

two yards he rowed me into the sunset,
past all pain. On everyone's lips was news

of my death but only that beloved couplet,
broken, on his:

"If there is a paradise on earth,
It is this, it is this, it is this."

AGHA SHAHID ALI (1949−2001)

HONEY

Light splashed its last spittle
on the window-panes,
like golden death-rattles the leaves
and the ivy a red
flame dying.
Love glowed phosphorescent,
drenched in the infernal colors
of the setting sun,
a pot of honey held
in his gleaming magic fingers.
Asteam, my body
smelled of the depths of the lake
of rotting vegetation
in the closed kitchen of time.
Come, come, he chuckled,
and coated my hairs
and the pink discs of my breasts.
Dense grey clouds
came rushing in
while amber
dripped from his nails.
Was it sweetness or menace
this diabolical anointing?
Some sort of evil was clinging to me,
some catastrophe blocking my pores one by one.

Heavy treacle oppressed me
and I hung in the void
like sticky flypaper
in the bare rooms of summer.
And you, glowing fiendishly,
your little pot empty,
a day-dreamer sitting
by the water
which mirrors you forever
with a garland of honey-colored
sunsets in your hair.

KATERINA ANGHELAKI-ROOKE (1939—2020)   181
TRANSLATED BY THE POET
AND JACKIE WILLCOX

SUGAR

Secret boxes
and bags stashed

in the back
of a never-used oven

or hidden behind pillows
on her smoke-filled settee:

the chocolate cups
and fudge-filled cakes

she numbered
and guarded.

Soil-dark palmfuls
and mouthfuls,

moist and eyeless.

Confections
sweating in plastic,

crowded in the dark
beneath her bed.

Secret sugar
is sweeter and hotter.

Electricity licks
the tongue, a seethe

near suckling
that ruined her mouth.

Dear mother who starved
during the Depression

as rations snatched
her brother away.

Mother who hides
the sugar behind

the spoiled cream
of soft teeth.

"GIRL CAT"

Girl cat,
so thin
on barley and love.

184   BASHO (1644–94)
TRANSLATED BY LUCIEN STRYK and
TAKASHI IKEMOTO

LENTILS

Barely ten, I watch my aunt
pour the bag of raw seeds –

orange orbs spill down
to a silver tray, flat and wide.

Her fingers push pebbles
to one side, shove hair

behind her ears
as she works, bows over

the pile of grain, makes
dinner for the seven of us.

Handing me a shaker of salt,
my cue is the blink of her eye.

Her radish cheeks begin to glow
above the boiling pot. Quiet,

I watch the blackened yarn
of her brows, the dark olive

of her skin. Beauty marks,
moles map her arms.

A somber bird, a movie star –
I can't decide what she is.

Single and thin, Syrian-born,
she sorts, counts lentils.

And each day, not a word,
not a complaint through her lips,

just her hold on a wooden spoon,
apron tied tight behind her back,

stirring, stirring the boiled seeds,
always above an open flame.

From WEST BANK DIARY

5TH MARCH: KOBAR

A hand worn by the years
calls and recalls lost time

Almond trees recall a marriage
in an old woman's garden

Time carries no more the memory of dreams
nor the bitterness of the five layers of green almonds
nor the immemorial cooking with wild herbs
nor betrothals celebrated on a new floor
nor the habitual stillness of the donkey when the wind
     changes
nor the gait of a mother when settlers pass by
nor the son's last poem engraved in stone

A black hole between the few teeth left
tells a story of a family in pieces

Under the shade of almond trees
a pair of earthy feet scatters specks of dust

YVES BERGER (1931–2004)
TRANSLATED BY JOHN BERGER

187

THE LICORICE FIELDS AT PONTEFRACT

In the licorice fields at Pontefract
My love and I did meet
And many a burdened licorice bush
Was blooming round our feet;
Red hair she had and golden skin,
Her sulky lips were shaped for sin,
Her sturdy legs were flannel-slack'd
The strongest legs in Pontefract.

The light and dangling licorice flowers
Gave off the sweetest smells;
From various black Victorian towers
The Sunday evening bells
Came pealing over dales and hills
And tanneries and silent mills
And lowly streets where country stops
And little shuttered corner shops.

She cast her blazing eyes on me
And plucked a licorice leaf;
I was her captive slave and she
My red-haired robber chief.
Oh love! for love I could not speak,
It left me winded, wilting, weak,
And held in brown arms strong and bare
And wound with flaming ropes of hair.

188   JOHN BETJEMAN (1906–84)

THE BEAN EATERS

They eat beans mostly, this old yellow pair.
Dinner is a casual affair.
Plain chipware on a plain and creaking wood,
Tin flatware.

Two who are Mostly Good.
Two who have lived their day,
But keep on putting on their clothes
And putting things away.

And remembering . . .
Remembering, with twinklings and twinges,
As they lean over the beans in their rented back room
that is full of beads and receipts and dolls and
cloths, tobacco crumbs, vases and fringes.

BEANS WITH GARLIC

this is important enough:
to get your feelings down,
it is better than shaving
or cooking beans with garlic.
it is the little we can do
this small bravery of knowledge
and there is of course
madness and terror too
in knowing
that some part of you
wound up like a clock
can never be wound again
once it stops.
but now
there's a ticking under your shirt
and you whirl the beans with a spoon,
one love dead, one love departed
another love . . .
ah! as many loves as beans
yes, count them now
sad, sad
your feelings boiling over flame,
get this down.

BEANS IN BLOSSOM

The south-west wind, how pleasant in the face
It breathes, while sauntering in a musing pace
I roam these new-ploughed fields, and by the side
Of this old wood where happy birds abide
And the rich blackbird through his golden bill
Utters wild music when the rest are still:
Now luscious comes the scent of blossomed beans
That o'er the path in rich disorder leans,
Mid which the bees in busy songs and toils
Load home luxuriantly their yellow spoils;
The herd cows toss the molehills in their play;
And often stand the stranger's steps at bay
Mid clover blossoms red and tawny-white,
Strong-scented with the summer's warm delight.

JOHN CLARE (1793–1864)

COFFEE BREAK

It was Christmastime,
the balloons needed blowing,
and so in the evening
we sat together to blow
balloons and tell jokes,
and the cool air off the hills
made me think of coffee,
so I said, "Coffee would be nice,"
and he said, "Yes, coffee
would be nice," and smiled
as his thin fingers pulled
the balloons from the plastic bags;
so I went for coffee,
and it takes a few minutes
to make the coffee
and I did not know
if he wanted cow's milk
or condensed milk,
and when I came out
to ask him, he was gone,
just like that, in the time
it took me to think,
cow's milk or condensed;
the balloons sat lightly
on his still lap.

HERBS FROM TIBET AND THE HIMALAYAS

My daughter brought me a gift from Mumbai.
A green pillow full of different herbs.
There's Matricaria camomila, Brassica nigra,
Cinnamomum camphora, Mentha arvensis,
Zingiber officinale, Nardostachys jatamansi.
Cold and severe are their names in Latin tongue.
That pillow I'm supposed to put inside my pillow,
so that my sleep will be harder and deeper,
penetrated by the scent and power of these herbs.
The grass in my yard was cut with sharp scythes,
or it was sucked by gas or electric lawn mowers.
I know, grasses end up as yellow haystacks,
as bales, or pulled clumps of earth.
I watched haystacks traveling to beautiful Čačak.
Fires devour them and turn them into black and
      gray ashes.
Perhaps, we human are like stalks of grass
which the wind from the north and south bends
      as they grow high.
We don't look like green clumps,
though there's even that within us.
Medicinal herbs, wild grasses out of which green
      juices flow like blood,
stalks of grass we chew or feed to the animals,

the grasses of Walt Whitman, the grasses of
      childhood, sea grasses,
the fur of the earth that dug its claws in the soil.
Like the air shifting, light smoke dispersing.
What quivers and thickly sprouts and flourishes in
      dreams.
So like those we feed our souls with, dreams,
in which we are little stones on the water bottom.

MILAN DJORDJEVIĆ (1954–)
TRANSLATED BY CHARLES SIMIC

PARSLEY

1. *The Cane Fields*

There is a parrot imitating spring
in the palace, its feathers parsley green.
Out of the swamp the cane appears

to haunt us, and we cut it down. El General
searches for a word; he is all the world
there is. Like a parrot imitating spring,

we lie down screaming as rain punches through
and we come up green. We cannot speak an R –
out of the swamp, the cane appears

and then the mountain we call in whispers *Katalina*.
The children gnaw their teeth to arrowheads.
There is a parrot imitating spring.

El General has found his word: *perejil*.
Who says it, lives. He laughs, teeth shining
out of the swamp. The cane appears

in our dreams, lashed by wind and streaming.
And we lie down. For every drop of blood

there is a parrot imitating spring.
Out of the swamp the cane appears.

2. *The Palace*

The word the general's chosen is parsley.
It is fall, when thoughts turn
to love and death; the general thinks
of his mother, how she died in the fall
and he planted her walking cane at the grave
and it flowered, each spring stolidly forming
four-star blossoms. The general

pulls on his boots, he stomps to
her room in the palace, the one without
curtains, the one with a parrot
in a brass ring. As he paces he wonders
Who can I kill today. And for a moment
the little knot of screams
is still. The parrot, who has traveled

all the way from Australia in an ivory
cage, is, coy as a widow, practising
spring. Ever since the morning
his mother collapsed in the kitchen
while baking skull-shaped candies

196

for the Day of the Dead, the general
has hated sweets. He orders pastries
brought up for the bird; they arrive

dusted with sugar on a bed of lace.
The knot in his throat starts to twitch;
he sees his boots the first day in battle
splashed with mud and urine
as a soldier falls at his feet amazed –
how stupid he looked! – at the sound
of artillery. *I never thought it would sing*
the soldier said, and died. Now

the general sees the fields of sugar
cane, lashed by rain and streaming.
He sees his mother's smile, the teeth
gnawed to arrowheads. He hears
the Haitians sing without R's
as they swing the great machetes:
Katalina, they sing, *Katalina*,

mi madle, mi amol en muelte. God knows
his mother was no stupid woman; she
could roll an R like a queen. Even
a parrot can roll an R! In the bare room
the bright feathers arch in a parody
of greenery, as the last pale crumbs

disappear under the blackened tongue. Someone
calls out his name in a voice
so like his mother's, a startled tear
splashes the tip of his right boot.
My mother, my love in death.
The general remembers the tiny green sprigs
men of his village wore in their capes
to honor the birth of a son. He will
order many, this time, to be killed

for a single, beautiful word.

PRECIOSA LIKE A LAST CUP OF COFFEE

for my grandmother, Luisa Roig, 1908–1997
Carolina, Puerto Rico

Tata says her wheelchair
has been stolen by the nurses.
She hallucinates the ceiling fan
spinning closer, the vertigo
of a plummeting helicopter,
but cannot raise her hands
against the blades. Her legs jerk
with the lightning that splits trees.
She scolds her dead sister,
who studies Tata's face
from a rocking chair by the bed
but does not answer.
The grandchildren are grateful
for the plastic diaper, the absence of bedsores.

Tata's mouth collapses without teeth;
her words are miners blackened in the hole.
Now a word pushes out: *café.*
No coffee for her, or she won't eat,
says the nurse.

Tata craves more than a puddle
in a styrofoam cup:
the coffee farm in Utuado, 1928,
the mountains hoisting a harvest of clouds,
the beans a handful of planets,
the spoon in the cup a silver oar,
and the roosters' bickering choir.

But no coffee today.
Cousin Bernice crawls into the bed,
stretches her body across Tata's body
like a drowsy lover, mouth hovering
before her grandmother's eyes
as she chants the word: *Preciosa*.

Preciosa like the song,
chorus brimming from a kitchen radio
on West 98th Street after the war,
splashing down the fire escape,
preciosa te llaman:
an island from the sky
or a last cup of coffee.
Tara repeats: *Preciosa*.

The song bathes her tongue.

WHEN OATS WERE REAPED

That day when oats were reaped, and wheat was ripe,
    and barley ripening,
The road-dust hot, and the bleaching grasses dry,
I walked along and said,
While looking just ahead to where some silent
    people lie:

"I wounded one who's there, and now know well
    I wounded her;
But, ah, she does not know that she wounded me!"
And not an air stirred,
Nor a bill of any bird; and no response accorded she.

THOMAS HARDY (1840–1928)

MUSTARD

Down at the lake we looked about us,
saw tares growing among the wheat,
saw fishermen at their nets,
saw the mustard's yellow blossoms,
pods bursting at the ends of stiff stems.

In dry graves its seeds have passed
millennia like minutes. Brought to light again,
these sprout in new tears. Tares, wheat,
fishermen still at their nets
under the golden sun, and mustard, for us

to taste the world's sorrow never grown old,
wisdom powdered to bloom on the tongue.

GHIRARDELLI: SAN FRANCISCO

> *"Studies show women crave chocolate more than any other food."*
>
> — newspaper clipping

At the start of the 17th century, pious
Mexican women sipped hot chocolate in church.
Bittersweet warmth filled their earthly bodies,

& their spirits levitated above the cloistered
drone of mass. In their eyes, the transported
glassiness of sexual gratification. Jealous

of such passion, the bishop forbade the practice.
His imminent death was bliss, poison slipped
into his own bowl of cocoa before matins.

Montezuma thought it an aphrodisiac & quaffed
dozens of goblets a day. Bronze & doomed,
in the throes of ecstasy he'd picture the certain

swoop & rise of condors behind the shut
wings of his eyelids. At Fisherman's Wharf,
I buy a sampler box for Valentine's Day,

anticipate your teeth marks on every piece.
The one shaped & grooved like a seashell
might cause you to grow unpredictable

as the Pacific. Inside the perfect, dark square,
the tropical swell of coconut or *oh, please,*
yes sugar drift of caramel. Will you place

a wafer laced with praline on my tongue?
Back from a New World, I'll come like Columbus
to Fernando's court & offer the innocent gift.

"FUNNY, ISN'T IT"

Funny, isn't it
to see a big hand of a man
eating an acorn

IPPEKIRO (1887–1946)

TRANSLATED BY SOICHI FURUTA

NOTES ON THE PEANUT
for the Poet David Henderson

Hi there. My name is George
Washington
Carver.
If you will bear with me
for a few minutes I
will share with you
a few
of the 30,117 uses to which
the lowly peanut has been put
by me
since yesterday afternoon.
If you will look at my feet you will notice
my sensible shoelaces made from unadulterated
peanut leaf composition that is biodegradable
in the extreme.
To your left you can observe the lovely Renoir
masterpiece reproduction that I have cleverly
pieced together from several million peanut
shell chips painted painstakingly so as to
accurately represent the colors of the original!
Overhead you will spot a squadron of Peanut B-52
Bombers flying due west.
I would extend my hands to greet you
at this time

206

except for the fact that I am holding a reserve
supply of high energy dry roasted peanuts
guaranteed to accelerate protein assimilation
precisely documented by my pocket peanut calculator;

May I ask when did you last contemplate the
     relationship
between the expanding peanut products industry
and the development of post-Marxian economic
     theory
which (Let me emphasize) need not exclude moral
     attrition
of prepuberty
polymorphic
prehensible skills within the population age sectors
of 8 to 15?
I hope you will excuse me if I appear to be staring
     at you
through these functional yet high fashion and
     prescriptive
peanut contact lenses providing for the most
minute observation of your physical response to all
     of this
ultimately nutritional information.
Peanut butter peanut soap peanut margarine peanut
brick houses and house and field peanut *per se* well
illustrate the diversified

potential of this lowly leguminous plant
to which you may correctly refer
also
as the goober the pindar the groundnut
and ground pea/let me
interrupt to take your name down on my
pocket peanut writing pad complete with matching
peanut pencil that only 3 or 4
chewing motions of the jaws will sharpen
into pyrotechnical utility
and no sweat.
Please:
Speak right into the peanut!

Your name?

AN INSIDER'S VIEW OF THE GARDEN

How can I help but admire the ever perseverant
unquenchable dill
that sways like an unruly crowd at a soccer match
waving its lacy banners
where garlic belongs or slyly invading a hill
of Delicata squash –
how can I help but admire such ardor? I seek it

as bees the flower's core, hummingbirds
the concocted sugar water
that lures them to the feeder in the lilacs.
I praise the springy mane
of untamed tendrils asprawl on chicken wire
that promise to bring forth
peas to overflow a pillowcase.

Some days I adore my coltish broccolis,
the sketchbook beginnings
of their green heads still encauled, incipient trees
sprung from the Pleistocene.
Some days the leeks, that Buckingham Palace patrol
and the quarter-mile of beans
– green, yellow, soy, lima, bush and pole –

demand applause. As do dilatory parsnips,
a ferny dell of tops
regal as celery. Let me laud onion that erupts
slim as a grass stem
then spends the summer inventing its pungent tulip
and the army of brussels sprouts
extending its spoon-shaped leaves over dozens of
     armpits

that conceal what are now merely thoughts, mere
     nubbins
needing long ripening.
But let me lament my root-maggot-raddled radishes
my bony and bored red peppers
that drop their lower leaves like dancehall strippers
my cauliflowers that spit
out thimblesize heads in the heat and take beetles
     to bed.

O children, citizens, my wayward jungly dears
you are all to be celebrated
plucked, transplanted, tilled under, resurrected here
– even the lowly despised
purslane, chickweed, burdock, poke, wild poppies.
For all of you, whether eaten or extirpated
I plan to spend the rest of my life on my knees.

A DISUSED SHED IN CO. WEXFORD

Let them not forget us, the weak souls among the asphodels.
— Seferis, *Mythistorema*

for J. G. Farrell

Even now there are places where a thought might grow —
Peruvian mines, worked out and abandoned
to a slow clock of condensation,
an echo trapped for ever, and a flutter
of wildflowers in the lift-shaft,
Indian compounds where the winds dance
and a door bangs with diminished confidence,
lime crevices behind rippling rain barrels,
dog corners for bone burials;
and in a disused shed in Co. Wexford,

deep in the grounds of a burnt-out hotel,
among the bathtubs and the washbasins
a thousand mushrooms crowd to a keyhole.
This is the one star in their firmament
or frames a star within a star.
What should they do there but desire?
So many days beyond the rhododendrons
with the world revolving in its bowl of cloud,
they have learnt patience and silence
listening to the rooks querulous in the high wood.

They have been waiting for us in a foetor
of vegetable sweat since civil war days,
since the gravel-crunching, interminable departure
of the expropriated mycologist.
He never came back, and light since then
is a keyhole rusting gently after rain.
Spiders have spun, flies dusted to mildew
and once a day, perhaps, they have heard something –
a trickle of masonry, a shout from the blue
or a lorry changing gear at the end of the lane.

There have been deaths, the pale flesh flaking
into the earth that nourished it;
and nightmares, born of these and the grim
dominion of stale air and rank moisture.
Those nearest the door grow strong –
'Elbow room! Elbow room!"
The rest, dim in a twilight of crumbling
utensils and broken pitchers, groaning
for their deliverance, have been so long
expectant that there is left only the posture.

A half century, without visitors, in the dark –
poor preparation for the cracking lock
and creak of hinges; magi, moonmen,
powdery prisoners of the old regime,
web-throated, stalked like triffids, racked by drought

and insomnia, only the ghost of a scream
at the flash-bulb firing squad we wake them with
shows there is life yet in their feverish forms.
Grown beyond nature now, soft food for worms,
they lift frail heads in gravity and good faith.

They're begging us, you see, in their wordless way,
to do something, to speak on their behalf
or at least not to close the door again.
Lost people of Treblinka and Pompeii!
"Save us, save us," they seem to say,
"let the god not abandon us
who have come so far in darkness and in pain.
We too had our lives to live.
You with your light meter and relaxed itinerary,
let not our naive labours have been in vain!"

THE RECIPE

She believed it would strengthen the blood,
the soup my grandmother Mary made:
nettle, onion, parsley, thyme and spud —

each spring when the nettle tips appeared
in clumps the rough end of the back yard.
I, a willing and complicit ward,

dogged her footsteps. Thus to learn the hard
way what a nettle was, to learn that good
comes sleeved in pain, had best be suffered.

RICE

It grew in the black mud.
It grew under the tiger's orange paws.
Its stems thinner than candles, and as straight.
Its leaves like the feathers of egrets, but green.
The grains cresting, wanting to burst.
Oh, blood of the tiger.

I don't want you just to sit down at the table.
I don't want you just to eat, and be content.
I want you to walk out into the fields
where the water is shining, and the rice has risen.
I want you to stand there, far from the white
    tablecloth.
I want you to fill your hands with the mud, like a
    blessing.

MARY OLIVER (1935–2019)

THE CINNAMON PEELER

If I were a cinnamon peeler
I would ride your bed
and leave the yellow bark dust
on your pillow.

Your breasts and shoulders would reek
you could never walk through markets
without the profession of my fingers
floating over you. The blind would
stumble certain of whom they approached
though you might bathe
under rain gutters, monsoon.

Here on the upper thigh
at this smooth pasture
neighbour to your hair
or the crease
that cuts your back. This ankle.
You will be known among strangers
as the cinnamon peeler's wife.

I could hardly glance at you
before marriage
never touch you
– your keen nosed mother, your rough brothers.

I buried my hands
in saffron, disguised them
over smoking tar,
helped the honey gatherers . . .

When we swam once
I touched you in water
and our bodies remained free,
you could hold me and be blind of smell.
You climbed the bank and said

   this is how you touch other women
the grass cutter's wife, the lime burner's daughter.
And you searched your arms
for the missing perfume

   and knew

   what good is it
to be the lime burner's daughter
left with no trace
as if not spoken to in the act of love
as if wounded without the pleasure of a scar.

You touched
your belly to my hands
in the dry air and said
I am the cinnamon
peeler's wife. Smell me.

MUSHROOMS

Overnight, very
Whitely, discreetly,
Very quietly

Our toes, our noses
Take hold on the loam,
Acquire the air.

Nobody sees us,
Stops us, betrays us;
The small grains make room.

Soft fists insist on
Heaving the needles,
The leafy bedding,

Even the paving.
Our hammers, our rams,
Earless and eyeless,

Perfectly voiceless,
Widen the crannies,
Shoulder through holes. We

Diet on water,
On crumbs of shadow,
Bland-mannered, asking

Little or nothing.
So many of us!
So many of us!

We are shelves, we are
Tables, we are meek,
We are edible,

Nudgers and shovers
In spite of ourselves.
Our kind multiplies:

We shall by morning
Inherit the earth.
Our foot's in the door.

A BOWL OF COOKED RICE IN SOUP
for the late Moongu Lee

After the phone call telling me that he probably
    wouldn't live another day
I rushed to the station.
But I was hungry.
Hunger was what I first felt upon hearing of his
    imminent death,
which was shameful, but I was hungry.
Waiting for departure time, I wolfed down
a bowl of cooked rice in soup.
Emptying the cooked rice into the reddish soup
I remembered the bowl of cooked rice in soup he
    gave me
on the mountain slope where we watched the lowering
    of the coffin.
I usually met him at funerals.
He never refused to serve as master of ceremonies
but now he who "stood or walked too long" wanted
to lay his own tired body down and breathe.
While a man's well emptied and his body grew cold
I devoured, without tears,
a bowl of soup like the one he gave me that last time.
What's mixed into this besides rice and soup,
and why do people wolf it down
as if nothing's the matter.

I couldn't understand why before he left he bestowed
      on me
this simple food that needs no garnishment.
I couldn't put the cooling bowl down.

222   HEEDUK RA (1966–)
      TRANSLATED BY WON-CHUNG KIM and
      CHRISTOPHER MERRILL

NUT TRAIL

Breezy hillside.
Half way up clearing trail
I start picking up walnuts.

> Walnuts, chestnuts, wild grapes . . .
> Nut trail, mushroom trail . . .
> Animal trail, human trail . . .
> Finally the trail diffuses into blue heaven.

Grassy hilltop.
A Blooming flower in front of me.
Who and what are you?
No answer.

> Loudly I call the flower by my lover's name
> Caressing with finger tips
> I wish to give my hands to her.

Now she has hands, legs and smiling face,
And suddenly jumps over me,
Passes through a spider's web,
Comes down as walnut.

> Here, I got you.

NANAO SAKAKI (1923–2008)   223

LITTLE MUSHROOMS

So this is how the whole thing goes
by far the best are the little mushrooms
little mushrooms in the soup
nada nada nada nada
                fiuuuuu one little mushroom
this little green parsley in tuxedo
and darkness for a long time
then they run to get a cleaning lady
responsible for all of this
nothing nothing nothing nothing
                fiuuuuuuu one more little mushroom
healthy though
the blood is not so great
because she got hepatitis
Heavy heavy are these little mushrooms
heavy in the Holy Mother

224   TOMAŽ ŠALAMUN (1941−2014)
       TRANSLATED BY THE POET and PHILLIS LEVIN

MIDNIGHT IN THE FOREIGN FOOD AISLE

Dear Uncle, is everything you love foreign
or are you foreign to everything you love?
We're all animals and the body wants what it wants,
I know. The blonde said *Come in, take off*
your coat and what do you want to drink?
Love is not haram, but after years of fucking
women who cannot pronounce your name,
you find yourself in the foreign food aisle,
beside the turmeric and the saffron of mothers' hands,
pressing your face into the ground, praying
in a language you haven't used in years.

WARSAN SHIRE (1988–)   225

From THE SONG OF SONGS

An enclosed garden is my sister, my bride,
a hidden well, a sealed spring.

Your branches are an orchard
of pomegranate trees heavy with fruit,
flowering henna and spikenard,
spikenard and saffron, cane and cinnamon,
with every tree of frankincense,
myrrh and aloes,
all the rare spices.

You are a fountain in the garden,
a well of living waters
that stream from Lebanon.

226   SOLOMON (*c.* 970–31 BCE)
        TRANSLATED BY ARIEL BLOCH and
        CHANA BLOCH

From THE FAERIE QUEENE

In secret chamber of the bowels deep,
Where vital spirits do most quietly sleep,
And in the rivers of life, where they do creep,
She sought out herbs of wondrous might and steep.
And every one she knew by name and sight,
And knew their hidden powers and secret might.

(Book III, Canto VI, stanza 6)

With her two handmaids, she in secret took
A little bag of herbs, and medicines wise,
To heal the wounds of knight and ladies broke.
And first she tooke of Moly, good to chase
All hurtful spirits from the wounded place;
And of Vermilion, which doth quell the heat
Of fiery inflammations, and their bitter seat.
She tooke of Camphire, and of Calamint,
To make the wounded flesh to close and hint;
And of the gentle Sanguisuge, to stay
The bleeding veins, and stop the bloody sway.
She tooke of Myrrh, and of Mercurey's might,
To heal the inward wounds, and deadly night.
And of the sacred Treacle, she did take,
To drive away the venom, and the poison's stake.

(Book III, Canto VI, stanza 7–8)

EDMUND SPENSER (1552–99)   227

MAKING A ROUX

I am making a roux, like my mother, like my grand-
mother, like all the women whose shadows stretch
before and behind me. I am standing before the stove
stirring, and I wonder what they thought of as they
        stood
and stirred, as their hands went round and round
in this ancient gesture. I wonder
if they looked deep into it as I do, as if it could speak,
stared at this flour and grease come together,
this stuff that is base, thickener, nothing
you cook will ever cohere without it, this
stuff that must be cooked over the slowest fire,
this stuff that must be tended
until the heat turns it the color of nuts,
the color of the earth, the river,
the sweet color of some skins,
the color the roux gives up
to the dish it will thicken.

I am making a roux, like my mother, like my grand-
mother, it is so simple, this flour and grease
come together with its thick bready
flavor, like the two of us come together.

Let it be a good roux, a dark roux, let the cream,
the smoky glue, the sweat and dirt of us,
thicken some dish already seasoned,
already rich.

SHERYL ST. GERMAIN (1954−)

THE SWEETNESS OF LIFE

After the heavy rain we were able to tell about the
       mushrooms,
which ones made us sick, which ones had the dry
       bitterness,
which ones caused stomach pains and dizziness and
       hallucinations.

It was the beginning of religion again – on the river –
all the battles and ecstasies and persecutions
taking place beside the hackberries and the fallen
       locust.

I sat there like a lunatic,
weeping, raving, standing on my head, living
in three and four and five places at once.

I sat there letting the wild and domestic combine,
finally accepting the sweetness of life,
on my own mushy log,
in the white and spotted moonlight.

LYCHEE EXPRESS

What would the lovely Yang Guifei,
concubine to the emperor,
a Helen of China, have made
of our gleaming grocery stores,

always awash in berries, melons,
tangerines? Her passion for lychees,
rushed north by a chain of horsemen,
laid waste to a dynasty.

She must have understood,
at least upon the deadly finale,
the cost of transporting food
so fragile over so many *li*

for pleasure, not necessity,
while the kingdom faltered.
History wants a great beauty
to undermine a ruler

through human weakness.
And who with highest power
would deny his most-loved mistress
her longing for a flavor

available briefly, far away?
There's something classical
about her appetite, about the chain
of sweating couriers, thirsty, fearful

of bruising the delicate fruit.
It proves how far we've come,
those tiny stickers with PLUs
and far-flung nations of origin

so common, we decry the waste.
The good peasants of antiquity
always ate locally, if at the cost
of variety, and under tyranny.

Neither they nor we would refuse
a bunch of ripe lychees in December.
Neither they nor we get to choose
who would eat humbly, who like an emperor.

From A HUNDRED GOOD POINTS
OF HUSBANDRY

Ginger to purge, and to expel
Cold humors, and to make thee swell
In kitchen us'd, to make thee broth
To comfort stomach, and to move thy troth

*

To make thy garden flourish, and thy crops to grow
Observe the seasons, and the weather's ebb and flow
Plant thy seeds in season, and thy roots in time
And prune thy trees, and thy hedges, in their prime

*

To make thy kitchen flourish, and thy food to be sweet
Use herbs, and spices, to make thy dishes meet
Ginger, and pepper, and cloves, and mace
Shall make thy food, and thy drink, a wondrous pace

THOMAS TUSSER (1524—80)   233

THE SPICE-TREE

In the great house of God, where many rooms are,
And many spices, which the heavenly merchant
    doth prepare;
There stands a tree of spice, whose branches high
    and wide
Do bear the costly merchandise, which the world doth
    seek and buy.

The root of this fair tree doth in the earth descend,
And with the hidden waters, of God's rich love doth
    ascend;
The trunk doth rise in stature, and the branches
    spread in might,
And with the precious spices, doth the world's dark
    senses light.

The bark of this fair tree, doth represent to me
The outward, and visible means, of God's rich grace,
    and mercy free;
The sap, which doth ascend, and doth the branches
    nourish all,
Doth represent the inward, and the spiritual means,
    which God doth call.

And as the merchant doth, with skill, and art,
    and pains,
Prepare the spices, and doth make them fit,
    for men's gains;
So doth the heavenly merchant, with his own hand,
    and art,
Prepare, and make fit, the spices of his garden,
    and his heart.

And when the season comes, that they should be
    revealed,
He sends his Spirit, as a wind, that doth the spices
    yield;
And then the world doth see, and doth the spices buy,
And with their precious odors, doth the world's dark
    senses fly.

MUSHROOMS

we met them in the forest at a clearing:
two expeditions through the twilight
that mutely watched each other. between us,
    nervously,
the telegraph-hum of a mosquito swarm.

my grandmother was famous for her recipe
of *champignons farcis.* she locked it into
her grave. whatever is good, said she,
one fills with little more than just itself.

later in the kitchen we held the mushrooms
close to our ears and turned the stems –
waiting for the gentle clicking inside,
searching for the proper combination.

236 JAN WAGNER (1971–)
TRANSLATED BY DAVID KEPLINGER

NUTTING

It seems a day
(I speak of one from many singled out)
One of those heavenly days that cannot die;
When, in the eagerness of boyish hope,
I left our cottage-threshold, sallying forth
With a huge wallet o'er my shoulders slung,
A nutting-crook in hand; and turned my steps
Toward some far-distant wood, a Figure quaint,
Tricked out in proud disguise of cast-off weeds
Which for that service had been husbanded,
By exhortation of my frugal Dame –
Motley accoutrement, of power to smile
At thorns, and brakes, and brambles, – and, in truth,
More ragged than need was! O'er pathless rocks,
Through beds of matted fern, and tangled thickets,
Forcing my way, I came to one dear nook
Unvisited, where not a broken bough
Drooped with its withered leaves, ungracious sign
Of devastation; but the hazels rose
Tall and erect, with tempting clusters hung,
A virgin scene! – A little while I stood,
Breathing with such suppression of the heart
As joy delights in; and, with wise restraint
Voluptuous, fearless of a rival, eyed
The banquet; – or beneath the trees I sate

Among the flowers, and with the flowers I played;
A temper known to those who, after long
And weary expectation, have been blest
With sudden happiness beyond all hope.
Perhaps it was a bower beneath whose leaves
The violets of five seasons re-appear
And fade, unseen by any human eye;
Where fairy water-breaks do murmur on
For ever; and I saw the sparkling foam,
And – with my cheek on one of those green stones
That, fleeced with moss, under the shady trees,
Lay round me, scattered like a flock of sheep –
I heard the murmur and the murmuring sound,
In that sweet mood when pleasure loves to pay
Tribute to ease; and, of its joy secure,
The heart luxuriates with indifferent things,
Wasting its kindliness on stocks and stones,
And on the vacant air. Then up I rose,
And dragged to earth both branch and bough, with
    crash
And merciless ravage: and the shady nook
Of hazels, and the green and mossy bower,
Deformed and sullied, patiently gave up
Their quiet being: and, unless I now
Confound my present feelings with the past,
Ere from the mutilated bower I turned
Exulting, rich beyond the wealth of kings,

I felt a sense of pain when I beheld
The silent trees, and saw the intruding sky. –
Then, dearest Maiden, move along these shades
In gentleness of heart; with gentle hand
Touch – for there is a spirit in the woods.

MINT GATHERERS
for Niamh Morris

While you are off gathering mint,
we stain our fingers
with a fresher smell
in the long, narrow room –
its tiny window making
four perfect purple squares
out of the far-away mountain –
that room with the yellow blanketed bed
that holds us wrapped in heat and love
over the kitchen, below the Alpine spider,
our own spindly guard
and his soft cylindrical web
in the angle of the latticed door.

The house is ours for that brief time
while you are off gathering mint
in your neighbour's field high on the hill.
You raise your hand in the afternoon heat,
rub water across your cheek, can lick already
the green coolness on the roof of your mouth –
while we, back there, taste each other.
There are no words. The lizards lie still
in the cool of the old barn. The lime tree shades
the balcony where we rise at last to stand,

now waiting for you to return.
certain you'll hang from hooks
in the kitchen ceiling
a bunch of fresh mint leaves to dry
just below where we had lain.

THE WOMAN CLEANING LENTILS

A lentil – a lentil – lentils – a lentil – a pebble – a
    lentil – a lentil – a pebble
A green one – a black one – a green one – a black one
    – a pebble – a green lentil
A lentil next to a lentil, a pebble next to a lentil –
    suddenly a word – a word next to a lentil
Then words – a lentil – a word – a word next to a
    word – then a phrase
And word by word a witless wording – a wornout
    song – a washed out dream
Then a life – another life – a life next to a life – a
    lentil – a life
An easy life – a hard life – why easy – why hard
But lives next to each other – a life – then a word –
    then a lentil
A green one – a black one – a green one – a black one
    – a pain – a green song
A green lentil – a black one – a pebble – a lentil – a
    pebble – a pebble – a lentil

ZAHRAD (1924–2007)
    TRANSLATED BY RALPH SETIAN

ACKNOWLEDGMENTS

Thanks are due to the following copyright holders for permission to reprint:

AGHA SHAHID ALI: "The Last Saffron." Copyright © 1997 by Agha Shahid Ali, from *The Veiled Suite: The Collected Poems* by Agha Shahid Ali. Used by permission of the author and W. W. Norton & Company, Inc. YEHUDA AMICHAI: "Inside the Apple" from *The Selected Poetry of Yehuda Amichai*, edited and translated by Chana Bloch and Stephen Mitchell. University of California Press, 1996. Reproduced with permission of the Licensor through PLSclear. KAREN LEONA ANDERSON: "Asparagus" from *Receipt: Poems*. Copyright © 2016 by Karen Leona Anderson. Reprinted with the permission of The Permissions Company LLC on behalf of Milkweed Editions, milkweed.org. KATERINA ANGHELAKI-ROOKE: "Honey," translated by Katerina Anghelaki-Rooke and Jackie Willcox, from *Beings And Things On Their Own*. Copyright © 1986 by Katerina Anghelaki-Rooke. Reprinted with the permission of The Permissions Company, LLC on behalf of BOA Editions, Ltd., boaeditions.org. ANONYMOUS: From *Inanna: Queen of Heaven and Earth*, translated by Diane Wolkstein and Samuel Noah Kramer. Harper & Row, 1983. Translation copyright © The Estate of Diane Wolkstein. Reprinted with permission. ANONYMOUS: "A Riddle" (10th century), translated by Megan Cavell, from *The Exeter Book*. Translation copyright © by Megan Cavell. Reprinted with permission. ANTIPHILOS: "A quince preserved" by Antiphilos, translated by W. S. Merwin, in *Selected Translations 1968–1978*, Atheneum, 1979. Copper Canyon Press. The Wylie Agency. JIMMY SANTIAGO BACA: "Green Chile" by Jimmy Santiago Baca, from *Black Mesa Poems*, copyright © 1989 by Jimmy Santiago Baca. Reprinted by permission of New Directions Publishing Corp. PETER BALAKIAN: "Zucchini." Used with permission of University of

Chicago Press, from *No Sign*, University of Chicago Press, 2022; permission conveyed through Copyright Clearance Center, Inc. HADARA BAR-NADAV: "Sugar" from *The New Nudity*, Saturnalia Books, 2017. LORY BEDIKIAN: "Lentils" from *The Book of Lamenting*, Anhinga Press, 2011. Copyright © 2011 by Lory Bedikian. Reprinted with permission from Anhinga Press. GERARD BENSON: "Garlic" from *The Bradford Poems*, Smith/Doorstop Books, 2014. Reprinted with permission. YVES BERGER: Excerpt from *West Bank Diary*, translated by John Berger, first published in *Modern Poetry in Translation* (UK), 2014, Number 2. Reprinted with permission from Yves Berger. JOHN BETJEMAN: "The Licorice Fields at Pontefract" from *Collected Poems*, Hodder and Stoughton Limited, 2006. Reproduced with permission of the Licensor through PLSclear. Farrar, Straus and Giroux. EAVAN BOLAND: "The Pomegranate" from *In a Time of Violence* by Eavan Boland. Copyright © 1994 by Eavan Boland. Used by permission of W. W. Norton & Company, Inc. "The Pomegranate," from *New Selected Poems* by Eavan Boland. Used by permission of Carcanet Press. YVES BONNEFOY: "Les Pommes" from Yves Bonnefoy, *Début et fin de la neige* © Mercure de France, 1991. Reprinted with permission. "The Apples," translated by Sarah Lawson. Translation copyright © 2007 by Sarah Lawson. Translation first published on Poetry International, 2014. Reprinted with permission from Sarah Lawson. JOSEPH BRODSKY: "Cabbage and Carrot" from *Collected Poems in English*, Farrar, Straus and Giroux, 2000. GWENDOLYN BROOKS: "The Bean Eaters" from *Blacks*, Third World Press. Reprinted by consent of Brooks Permissions. CHARLES BUKOWSKI: "beans with garlic" from *Burning in Water, Drowning in Flame: Selected Poems 1955–1973* by Charles Bukowski. Copyright © 1963, 1964, 1965, 1966, 1967, 1968, 1974 by Charles Bukowski. Used by permission of HarperCollins Publishers. CIARAN CARSON: "Spraying the Potatoes," by kind permission of the author's Estate and The Gallery Press, Loughcrew, Oldcastle, County Meath, Ireland, from *Collected Poems: Volume One* (2023).

246

permission of the Licensor through PLSclear. ROSS GAY: "Autumn" by Ross Gay, originally published in *Orion Magazine*, and subsequently in *Lace & Pyrite: Letters from Two Gardens* by Ross Gay and Aimee Nezhukumatathil, Get Fresh Books, 2022 (www. gfbpublishing.org). Reprinted with permission from the poets. KARIN GOTTSHALL: "The Raspberry Room" from Karin Gottshall, *Crocus* (© 2007 Fordham University Press). Reprinted with permission. ROBERT HASS: "Poem with a Cucumber in It" from *Time and Materials: Poems 1997–2005* by Robert Hass. Copyright © 2007 by Robert Hass. Used by permission of HarperCollins Publishers. SEAMUS HEANEY: "Blackberry-Picking" from *Opened Ground: Selected Poems 1966–1996* by Seamus Heaney. Published by Faber and Faber Ltd., 1998. Reprinted with permission. "Blackberry-Picking" from *Opened Ground: Selected Poems 1966–1996* by Seamus Heaney, Farrar, Straus and Giroux, 1998. MIGUEL HERNÁNDEZ: "Your heart? – it is a frozen orange," translated by Robert Bly, from *The Winged Energy of Delight: Selected Translations* by Robert Bly. Copyright © 2004 by Robert Bly. Used by permission of HarperCollins Publishers. *The Winged Energy of Delight: Selected Translations* by Robert Bly. Copyright © 2004 by Robert Bly. Reprinted by permission of Georges Borchardt, Inc., on behalf of the author's estate. All rights reserved. WILLIAM HEYEN: "Mustard," originally published in *Nature*, Cyberwit (India), 2020, and subsequently in *Nature: Selected & New Poems*, Mammoth Books (USA), 2024. Reprinted with permission from the poet. NAZIM HIKMET: "The Cucumber" from *Poems of Nazim Hikmet*. Translation copyright © 1994 by Randy Blasing and Mutlu Konuk. Reprinted with the permission of Persea Books, Inc. (New York), www. perseabooks.com. All rights reserved. JANE HIRSHFIELD: "Green-Striped Melons" from *Come, Thief: Poems* by Jane Hirshfield, copyright © 2011 by Jane Hirshfield. Used by permission of Alfred A. Knopf, an imprint of the Knopf Doubleday Publishing Group, a division of Penguin Random House LLC. All rights reserved.

"Green-Striped Melons" from *The Asking: New and Selected Poems* (Bloodaxe Books, 2024). Reproduced with permission of Bloodaxe Books. www.bloodaxebooks.com @bloodaxebooks (twitter/facebook) #bloodaxebooks. JOHN HOPPENTHALER: "Ghirardelli: San Francisco" from *Lives of Water*. Copyright © 2002 by John Hoppenthaler. Reprinted with the permission of The Permissions Company, LLC on behalf of Carnegie Mellon University Press, cmu.edu/universitypress. TED HUGHES: "Apple Dumps" from *New Selected Poems 1957–1994*, published by Faber and Faber Ltd., 1995. Reprinted with permission. "Apple Dumps" from *Selected Poems 1957–1994*, published by Farrar, Straus and Giroux, 2002. IPPEKIRO: "Funny, isn't it," translated by Soichi Furuta, from *Cape Jasmine and Pomegranate*, Grossman Publishers, a division of Penguin Random House LLC. KOBAYASHI ISSA: "The Man Pulling Radishes," translated by Robert Hass, from *The Essential Haiku: Versions of Basho, Buson, and Issa*, edited and with verse translations by Robert Hass. Translation copyright © 1994 by Robert Hass. Used by permission of HarperCollins Publishers. "The Man Pulling Radishes," translated by Robert Hass, from *The Essential Haiku: Versions of Basho, Buson, and Issa* (Ecco, 2013; Bloodaxe Books, 2013). Reproduced with permission of Bloodaxe Books. www.bloodaxebooks.com @bloodaxebooks (twitter/facebook) #bloodaxebooks. MAHMOOD JAMAL: "Apples and Mangoes" from *Sugar-Coated Pill: Selected Poems*, published by Word Power Books, Edinburgh. The Estate of Mahmood Jamal. JUNE JORDAN: "Notes on the Peanut" from *We're On: A June Jordan Reader* (Alice James Books, 2017). Copyright © 2017 by Christopher D. Meyer. All rights reserved. Reprinted by permission of the Frances Goldin Literary Agency. HÉDI KADDOUR: "Fruit on the Windowsill," translated by Marilyn Hacker, from *Treason: Poems by Hédi Kaddour*, translated by Marilyn Hacker, Yale University Press, 2010. Gallimard. ILYA KAMINSKI: "1942." Reprinted with permission of the author. PATRICK KAVANAGH: "Spraying the Potatoes" by

Momo's Press, 1979, and subsequently by Stop Press, 2020. Reprinted by permission of Joan Blackburn. GEORGE MACBETH: "To Preserve Figs" from *Selected Poems*, Enitharmon Press, 2023. Reprinted with permission. DEREK MAHON: "A Disused Shed in Co. Wexford." By kind permission of the author's Estate and The Gallery Press, Loughcrew, Oldcastle, County Meath, Ireland from *The Poems: 1961–2020* (2021). OSIP MANDELSTAM: "The shy speechless sound," translated by Clarence Brown and W. S. Merwin, from *Selected Poems*, Atheneum. Simon & Schuster. The Wylie Agency. DONNA MASINI: "Two Grapefruits" from *Turning to Fiction: Poems* by Donna Masini. Copyright © 2004 by Donna Masini. Used by permission of W. W. Norton & Company, Inc. SHARA MCCALLUM: "Planting" from *Song of Thieves* by Shara McCallum, © 2003. Reprinted by permission of the University of Pittsburgh Press. MEDBH MCGUCKIAN: "The Seed-Picture." By kind permission of the author and The Gallery Press, Loughcrew, Oldcastle, County Meath, Ireland from *The Flower Master* (1993). "The Seed Picture," from *The Unfixed Horizon: New Selected Poems* (2015), Wake Forest University Press. Reprinted with permission. PAULA MEEHAN: "The Recipe" from *As If By Magic*, Dedalus Press. Reprinted by kind permission of The Dedalus Press, Dublin, Ireland (www.dedaluspress.com). "The Recipe" from *As If By Magic: Selected Poems* (2021), Wake Forest University Press. Reprinted with permission. AGI MISHOL: "Olive Tree" from *Look There: New and Selected Poems*, translated by Lisa Katz. Copyright © 2006 by Agi Mishol. Translation copyright © 2006 by Lisa Katz and The Institute for the Translation of Hebrew Literature. Reprinted with the permission of The Permissions Company, LLC on behalf of Graywolf Press, Minneapolis, Minnesota, graywolfpress.org. The Institute for the Translation of Hebrew Literature. EUGENIO MONTALE: "The Lemons," translated by Jonathan Galassi, from *Collected Poems 1920–1954*, Farrar, Straus and Giroux, 1998. PAMELA MORDECAI: "Not for Everybody" by Pamela Mordecai, from

The editors want to express their gratitude to Zafira Demiri for her research assistance.